MASSIVE SMALL

THE OPERATING PROGRAMME
FOR SMART URBANISM

beta version
© 2011

D1421886

KELVIN CAMPBELL

urbanexchange

Urban Exchange began as a collaboration between Kelvin Campbell and Robert Cowan, and has now matured into the publishing arm of Urban Initiatives.

Prior publications include:

The Cities Design Forgot (1995, sponsored by Chesterton, English Partnerships, inner city Enterprises, and Richard and Ruth Rogers, now out in print) called for collaboration in the processes of urban design and regeneration.

The Connected City (1997 sponsored by Coin Street Community Builders and the space organisation) focused on ways of connecting both the city's fabric and the people who shape it. The method it proposed for preparing city and neighborhood action plans became the basis for urban design Alliance's now widely used Placecheck method.

Re:urbanism – A Challenge to the Urban Summit (2002) was sponsored by Yorkshire Forward and provided an agenda for debate around urban renaissance. Available from Urban Exchange on request.

Smart Urbanism is the online community dedicated to sustainable urbanism and social innovation that collaborated in the editing and content of this book.

MASSIVE SMALL is published by Urban Exchange c/o Urban Initiatives Ltd.
1 Fitzroy Square, London, U.K. W1T 5HE

massivesmall.com

Photography courtesy of iStockphoto, Photonica, Urban Initiatives, unless otherwise credited.

Illustrations by Kelvin Campbell and Ke Wang of Urban Initiatives, unless otherwise credited.

Design by Christopher Freeman, Urban Initiatives.

Printed by Glennleigh Print, London, U.K.
+44 20 7437 4444
glennleigh.co.uk

ISBN 978-0-9568600-0-2

*To be in opposition is not to be a
nihilist. And there is no decent or
charted way of making a living at
it. It is something you are, and not
something you do.*

—Christopher Hitchens,
   "Letters to a Young Contrarian"

KELVIN CAMPBELL

Kelvin is a terminally-dissatisfied idealist
as well as a seasoned contrarian, so this book
comes as no surprise.

An architect/urban designer, he co-founded
Urban Initiatives, a highly regarded urban
design practice, and, more recently, the Smart
Urbanism Group: an active and growing online
community devoted to sustainable urbanism
and social innovation.

The lead author of 'By Design' (CABE) 2000,
the national policy document on urban design,
and the recent Mayor of London's 'Housing
Design Guide', he has published, edited and
written numerous books and articles on urban
design, including 'Re:Urbanism: A Challenge
to the Urban Summit', which pointed the way
to MASSIVE SMALL.

He is Visiting Professor in Urban Design at
the University of Westminster; was on CABE's
Design Review Committee and the Prince's
Foundation Advisory Panel; past Chairman of
the Urban Design Group; and a long time asses-
sor for the National Housing Design Awards.

Kelvin lives in London with his wife, Louise,
having moved there some 25 years ago, and is
still in awe of the city. He has a son, Andrew,
who is an active collaborator in the book.

BOOTING UP

"Never waste the opportunities offered by a good crisis."
—Machiavelli

"We are taking on the enemies of enterprise: Public sector procurement managers who think that the answer to everything is a big contract with a big business and who shut out millions of Britain's small and medium sized companies from a massive potential market."
—David Cameron MP

"Hope is definitely not the same thing as optimism. It is not the conviction that something will turn out well, but the certainty that something makes sense, regardless of how it turns out."
—Vaclav Havel

"What all this demonstrates is that design – no matter how great – won't cut it on its own. That, unsurprisingly, some of the problems in Britain today are too deep and complex for architects to fix single-handedly. Complex problems can never be tackled with one-dimensional solutions."
—Grant Shapps MP

"Have a bias toward action – let's see something happen now. You can break that big plan into small steps and take the first step right away."
—Indira Gandhi

"Instead of planning being seen as the forum and the discipline whereby people can shape the places where they live for the better, it has become a crucible for controversy and acrimony. We have proposals, which go back to first principles – not just tinkering with processes, but rebooting the way we think about planning altogether."
—Greg Clark MP

"We need innovative ideas that will reshape how we invest, build and deliver affordable homes in London and in return I'll put my land where my mouth is and show London is leading the way on delivering affordable homes for 2011 and beyond."
—Boris Johnson, Mayor of London

"It's simple; if it jiggles, it's fat."
—Arnold Schwarzenegger

A certain amount of opposition is a great help to a man.
Kites rise against, not with, the wind.

—Lewis Mumford

A hallmark of British culture is the love of opposition. If you like one sort of thing, there is an automatic assumption that you will dislike what is assumed to be the opposite. It is not enough for things merely to be different. If you like Bath you are not allowed to like Brasilia. Tea beats coffee. Classicism beats Modernism. Or, of course, vice versa.

The defining of everything by it's assumed opposite, or by definition by silo has had malign consequences for design. The separation of planning, architecture, traffic management and highways planning, each with their own political as well as historical and cultural hinterlands, has made it nearly impossible to undertake the sort of city planning we require for the 21st Century without resorting to tick boxes to this of that example of silo culture.

Planning, instead of dealing with things in the round, deals with separated elements of a larger problem or opportunity, in which it is difficult for the sum of the parts even to add up to their mathematical total, let alone exceed it. None of this has been helped by the assertion that design is an entirely unified activity and that the designing something small is simply a micro process of designing something big. The idea that designing a spoon is the same as designing a city is ludicrous for any number of reasons, but is positively dangerous in respect of the implication that a city is a big spoon, that a large thing is just a magnified version of a small thing.

In reality, size and scale have their own dynamic, which at some point make big things different in kind from small things. (Because they are different does not mean they are better or worse. It means they are different. Very tall skyscrapers are not simply big versions of shorter skyscrapers.) The question is how you keep the advantages of good small-scale environments while at the same time benefitting from the larger-scale.

Kelvin Campbell has had ample opportunity to ponder these issues, and this volume is a concentrate of observations from a busy professional life dealing with the apparently intractable. Its underlying message is that planning is a creative exercise in opening up beneficial futures, not the imposition of rigid predictions doomed to failure in a world of fractal change.

—Paul Finch, Chair: Design Council CABE Board

CONTENTS

*Cities are victims of processes, practices and myths
that render good urbanism stillborn. There are bugs
deep in the system. They will continue to frustrate
true urban renaissance unless they are dealt with
systematically and comprehensively.*

—Re:Urbanism, 2002

PROLOGUE

So... top-down, command-and-control doesn't work for us any more, does it? Those in power tell us that bottom-up is the better way of addressing the sustainable growth and change of our cities, towns and neighbourhoods. They may be right. Despite the boom of recent years, we haven't delivered the quality of place we all wished for. This book will show why we haven't had much success. It will show how we can learn from self-organising systems that we can find in traditional cities, in nature and in the Web, to develop a new and evolving paradigm. It will also show how new thinking has been applied in recent initiatives. Further, it will explore how our behaviours in planning, design and delivery will need to change to meet our new challenges.

A lot has changed since I wrote 'Re:Urbanism: A Challenge to the Urban Summit' with Rob Cowan in 2002. This was our rage at the limited and superficial thinking that prevailed in our planning, design and delivery systems of the time. Like some art house movie, our audience was limited. Most eyes and ears were closed to what we were saying.

At the time, our industry was riding on the wave of architectural euphoria – like a Hollywood blockbuster- just design it big and it will pull in the crowds. Now however, the agenda has significantly changed and the audience has widened. The old concerns are more valid than ever before and more items have been added. The bugs have burrowed deeper and, although we may have engineered a number of 'patches', the systems are now largely corrupted.

We know where we want to be. We know where we need to be. We know where we have to be. We have just not been able to get to these places. We still face enormous challenges: rapid population growth; climate change; economic globalisation; resource depletion and increasing prices; mass population movements from country to cities and from country to country; reduced biodiversity and damage to natural systems.

Put this all together with what McKinseys calls the 'New Normal' – the fundamental shifts in our economies; the changing social and cultural patterns of urban life; the rise of new technologies; and the new political imperatives – then the real challenges come into stark focus. Each of these challenges require us to develop a radical new approach to the way we design, build and live in cities if we are to get through the 21st century.

Smart Urbanism moves away from the same old 'place making' agenda to that of 'condition making' - a new way of planning, designing and delivering sustainable urbanism and social innovation in our districts, neighbourhoods and quarters. It is how urban design must change in this new world.

I will show how we can learn from the science of complexity and emergent systems and, using this thinking, attempt to describe a new way for delivering good urbanism. "Oh no! Not that hippy science again", I hear you groan. I know, but I will show how we have overlooked many of its important properties and how we can apply these in our new bottom-up world and post-industrial society. I will also show how we can learn from new thinking around open collaborative systems as an alternative to our rigid hierarchical models; how we can learn from choice architecture to guide positive change; and how we can draw inspiration from Jane Jacobs' old work to develop new solutions for our cities, towns and neighbourhoods.

Re:Urbanism set out an agenda for a debate. What people said was, "Good rant, but what are you going to do about it!" This time I have tried to make a proposition. It is not perfectly formed, so it still is a debate – but it does show a potential way forward. By opening the publication to a wider audience for editing, I have been able to include many diverse views and expand on some of the weaker points. This has been very useful in road testing some of these ideas and I thank those who helped.

MASSIVE SMALL, the theme expounded in this book, is the operating programme for 'Smart Urbanism', a working methodology for creating the conditions to make massive small change in our towns and cities. I will describe new thought processes in structuring cities, towns and their localities: districts, neighbourhoods and quarters; in public collaboration, infrastructure provision, neighbourhood formation and in housing development. And I will expand on new tools and techniques to facilitate these processes. I will also show you examples where my colleagues at Urban Initiatives and others have been pioneering work in this field.

You will still see remnants of Rob's stylish prose in this book. I have lifted many relevant sections of Re:Urbanism; expanded on them where needed and tweaked them where necessary to bring them up to date. The first three chapters [Theorem, Broken and Thinking] set the scene for the final chapter [Fix]. The tone of the last chapter is deliberately less blokey. As someone said it is 'more Monocle than Hackney'. I wanted it to be a more serious piece, so I apologise if I have slipped into the jargon of my profession. In many ways, if we agree with sentiments in the first three chapters, it could stand alone.

The book will make the case that the masterplan is not dead in a bottom-up world. It becomes even more important but must take different forms – it must now be more suggestive than prescriptive, more enabling than determining. We know we cannot dictate end states but we can release the ingenuity of collective thinking of man if we put the right conditions in place. Bottom-up is not the same as 'laissez faire', but it does mean letting the system govern itself as much as possible, letting it learn from its actions. If the processes and behaviours that are the essence of planning, design and delivery are to change to respond to the new agenda, the masterplan must look to the lightest touch, not the heavy hand of control. The masterplan becomes the 'microplan' – the means of enabling MASSIVE SMALL.

This book is not intended to be an academic dissertation. It is a sourcebook of ideas to explore potential outcomes and invite responses from an informed audience. As such, I have termed it my 'beta version', implying more testing has to be done. Like most work in progress, it is always emerging!

I have gained much insight from so many places and individuals over the years, but have forgotten where much of it came from. For avoidance of doubt, I am saying that all of the intelligence in this book has come from others and credit is due to many. I am merely the processor of this intelligence and have tinkered with some of its source codes. So, I have not followed the protocol of quoting every source. I have rather relied on a good bibliography at the back.

I have many to thank – the great old urban theorists whose words still inspire: Jane Jacobs, Christopher Alexander, Lewis Mumford and Fritz Schumacher; and the new writers whose thinking on complexity is so relevant to urbanism: John Maeda, Peter Miller, Philip Howard and Stephen Johnson. My gratitude is extended to two people whose opinions I really respect, Peter Bishop and Paul Finch, and for their wise words up front. Special thanks to Chris Freeman for his excellent graphic eye and patience in the face of trial and error on my part; to Oci Stott and Christopher Martin, who helped with proof-reading; and finally, to my colleagues at Urban Initiatives and Smart Urbanism for their support.

This book could not have happened without the valuable help of Wikipedia, the perfect researcher.

—Kelvin Campbell

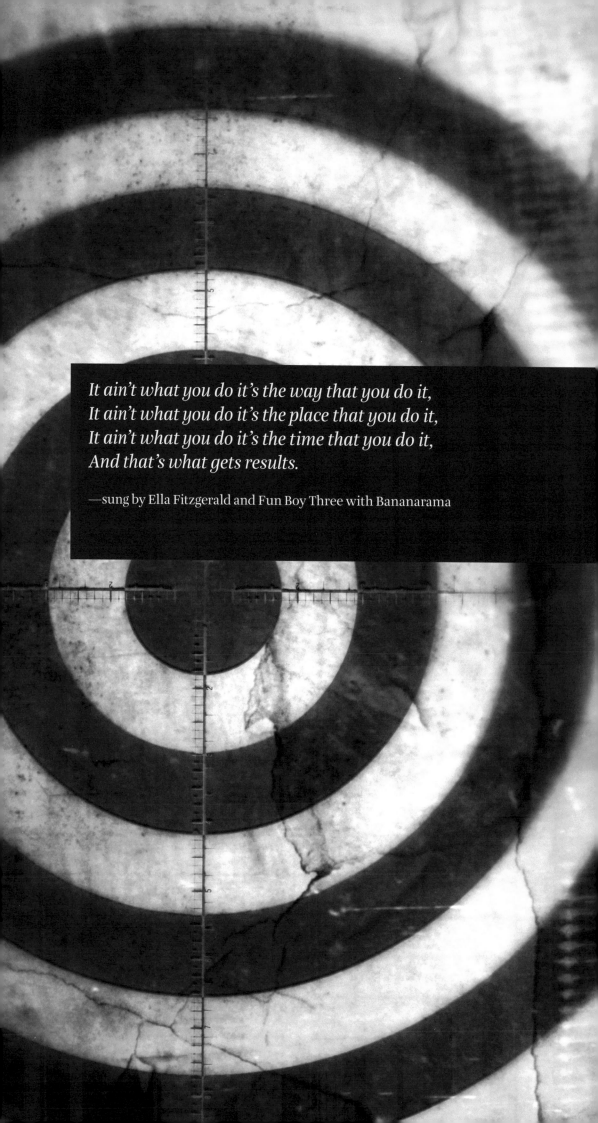

It ain't what you do it's the way that you do it,
It ain't what you do it's the place that you do it,
It ain't what you do it's the time that you do it,
And that's what gets results.

—sung by Ella Fitzgerald and Fun Boy Three with Bananarama

THEOREM

Social, cultural and demographic shifts have created the conditions and the demand for new thinking. The experience of city living is valued more than ever. In Britain, many of our cities are the product of an industrial society. Post-industrial society may not create urbanism in any familiar way, but it needs it more than ever. With capital and knowledge increasingly mobile, and technology allowing people to work and live apart, urbanism provides the means of bringing us together. The more our lives are lived through the global information network, the more we want to feel we belong to actual, physical neighbourhoods to which we can contribute as citizens. The new wealth-creators will move to, or stay in, cities or neighbourhoods whose built and natural environment offers them what they see as an attractive quality of life.

We need a new philosophy to guide practice and education in how to make great cities and neighbourhoods for the twenty-first century. Otherwise we will continue to make do with nothing more than patching up what we have or slavishly reproducing past forms. Without a philosophy to underpin good urbanism, governments will be frustrated in their attempts to implement its other social, economic and environmental policies.

This book spells out our ideas on our emerging theory, Smart Urbanism – a new paradigm that is evolving as we continue to work on it. Like every good theory, it has its own theorem. Like every good theorem, it is a proposition that can be proved or deduced from other propositions.

---

theorem: *[thee-er-uhm, theer-uhm] –noun*

1. *a theoretical proposition, statement, or formula embodying something to be proved from other propositions or formulas.*

2. *a rule or law, esp. one expressed by an equation or formula.*

3. *a proposition that can be deduced from the premises or assumptions of a system.*

4. *an idea, belief, method, or statement generally accepted as true or worthwhile without proof.*

The MASSIVE SMALL theorem states that:

The emergence of true urban life, and therefore a flourishing society and a healthy local economy, is inversely proportional to the bigness of the solution.

It holds that:

- The way we currently plan, design and deliver our towns and cities will not get us where we want to be... notwithstanding our efforts in recent years to improve city competitiveness, build stable communities and achieve sustainable development;

- The way we currently DO, LEARN and INFLUENCE social, economic and environmental development will not get us to where we need to be... often because we don't join all these activities up effectively;

- The way we currently organise our activities around single disciplines, specialisms and interests is completely inadequate when confronting the challenge of sustainable living, characterised as it is by systematic and cross-disciplinary connectivity;

- That we need new thinking, new metrics and new exemplars that will give us a far better evidence base and set of tools to move us from where we are now to where we have to be;

- That we need new fixes that will only emerge if we get to the root of what is 'broken' and realise the healing effect of new thinking [not same thinking] and effective tools to solve the problem; and

- That small changes to our current planning, design and delivery processes will make big differences to the outcomes of our cities, towns and their localities: districts, neighbourhoods and quarters.

Like every theorem, MASSIVE SMALL is a statement that can be demonstrated to be true by accepted arguments. This could be through an embodiment of general principles that makes it part of a larger theory or by deduction. Opening up our minds to new thinking enables us to do this.

The process of showing any theorem to be correct is called 'proof' and we know this is often 'in the eating'. The theorem only works if we recognise the state that we are in and if there is a will to allow change to occur. The proof therefore lies in those in power moving towards a more enabling culture: a condition that will allow a greater bottom-up collective response by multiple actors in the process of urban transformation: something that is on the cards.

This tongue-in-cheek slogan is written on a wall in Shoreditch in East London and could capture in a few words what we are going through today. There is an implied slant to it: that things are not working and are changing whether we like it or not. It also recognises the pain and challenge of change. We are all knee-deep in it!

What we are no doubt experiencing is the time of turbulence that afflicts societies once every hundred years where we see a new investigation of our societal norms and expressions (and the machinery of governance) that gives meaning to these norms and expressions – a moral and ideological reawakening of our basic senses that says 'we can do better'.

We are now moving well beyond Maslow's hierarchy of individual needs that starts with our natural instinct for survival and ends with self-actualisation – towards a value system that responds to our more evolved, higher order, collective needs. This means those that start with sense of belonging, social concern and need for collaborative interaction and move towards progress in the pursuit of success and transformation of society. Unfortunately all our levers for managing change are based around the individual and not the collective, with personal freedoms seemingly rated higher than collective social responsibility.

This means that we must have new metrics to measure and steer the ambitions of the theorem: a greater bottom-up response by the many to delivering MASSIVE SMALL change.

THE NEW NORMAL

New Normal is a term often used by McKinsey and other leading economists to define the conditions in a new post-credit crunch economy. It recognises that things will never be the same as before and for the doom and gloom merchants, the trend suggests two things: lowered expectations for economic activity, and a climate of austerity. The question is, "What will normal look like?" While no one can say how long the crisis will last, what we find on the other side will not look like the normal of recent years. The new normal will be shaped by a confluence of powerful forces – some arising directly from the financial crisis and some that were at work long before it began. For those who have recognised the power of the New Economy with all its potential: more start-ups, fewer giants and infinite opportunity.

As Chris Anderson, the editor of Wired Magazine states, 'the result is that the next new economy, the one rising from the ashes of this latest meltdown, will favour the small. Involuntary entrepreneurship is now creating tens of thousands of small businesses and a huge market of contract and freelance labour. Many will take full-time jobs again once they become available, but many others will choose not to. The crisis may have turned our economy into small pieces, loosely joined, but it will be the collective action of millions of workers hungry for change that keeps it that way."

The fragmentation of our economy points to a completely new way of looking at the pattern, grain and usage our cities. Small pieces fit within a big idea.

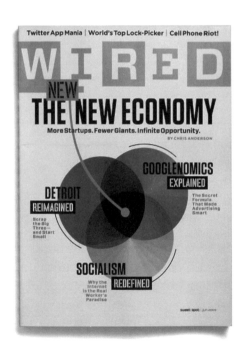

Kevin Kelly, author of the "New Economy" recognises a new emerging socialism at work. "Nearly every day another start-up proudly heralds a new way to harness community action. These developments suggest a steady move toward a sort of socialism uniquely tuned for a networked world. He notes that while old-school socialism was an arm of the state, digital socialism is socialism without the state. This new brand of socialism currently operates in the realm of culture and economics, rather than government – for now."

Anyone who believes exponential growth can go on forever in a finite world is either a madman or an economist.

—Kenneth Boulding, economist

THE NEW LOCAL

Localism usually describes social measures or trends that emphasise or value local and small-scale phenomena. This is in contrast to large, all-encompassing frameworks for action or belief. The UK government's new Localism Bill, launched in late 2010, takes this further to define a new form of governance: a radical shift of power from the centralised state to local communities. Big Government now becomes Big Society: people working together for the common good. It is about achieving collective goals in ways that are more diverse, more local and more personal. This comes with devolution of power to the neighbourhood and with it, the necessity to deal with the complexity of multiple actions. It is 'massive small' writ large.

A culture is unsalvageable if stabilising forces themselves become ruined and irrelevant. The collapse of one sustaining cultural institution enfeebles others, makes it more likely that others will give way... until finally the whole enfeebled, intractable contraption collapses.

—Jane Jacobs

If the New Normal is driving our thinking on a changed economy and Localism is driving thinking on changed governance of society, what is driving our urban design thinking on the social, cultural and physical dimension of our cities and neighbourhoods in this changing world? We are still using theorems that were evolved for a different world. They were relevant at the time of a burgeoning industrial economy and were a response to the problems that beset society at the time:

- poor health conditions and dirty smelly smokestacks that spawned the flight to the suburbs;

- jobs from the cradle to the grave that crystallised these places;

- investment and development processes that formalised the structure of the city and its component parts; and

- governance that reinforced the system.

These theorems are not fit for purpose in this new multiple action, highly mobile, responsive post-industrial world. They are ruined and irrelevant.

THREE BIG DRIVERS OF POLICY

No matter which political complexion, we know that there are still three big national policy agendas that drive our thinking on transformational change in our towns and cities: ensuring city competitiveness; building stable communities; and achieving sustainable development.

All three are intrinsically linked, all three are mutually supportive and all three have laudable aims. The trouble is we are not delivering any of these drivers effectively.

CITY COMPETITIVENESS

Let's first look at the ambition of city competitiveness. If 'attracting and retaining talent' is set out in bold on the opening statement on any city's economic strategy, do we really understand the values and needs of 'talent'? What is 'talent' and how does it succeed and excel? How does 'talent' want to work and live out its life in towns and cities? It certainly isn't in the products we have been creating in recent years. When it assesses the success of those cities that attract talent, Monocle magazine's Cities' Index points to a different set of metrics than those that drive our current way of shaping places. Many of these metrics are the complex intangibles of life: innovation, culture, social activity, and coolness.

> *Increasingly, we live in a world where cities compete for people, and businesses follow. This trend has largely been ignored by many cities, which are still focused on business climate and tax incentives. But I think the big question businesses will ask in the years to come is going to be 'Can I hire talented people in this city?' Cities need to be able to answer 'yes' to succeed.*

—Carol Coletta (CEOs for Cities)

True talent usually has a hunger to learn and innovate, and when you create an environment where talent lives and works in close proximity, you are on your way to building a knowledge economy. Their work influences each other and stimulates them towards innovation. If you introduce the social networks of cities, you have just created a multiplier effect and increased innovation exponentially, further fuelling the growth of the knowledge economy. Good cities, towns and neighbourhoods attract talent. Talent attracts talent.

Where are we making the great urban quarters that 'talent' wants to work in, can invest in, can innovate? Where can a new business start up; a place where the lowest rung on the economic ladder is not too high – the home of the new economy? Where are the great streets that talent wants to walk down or sit on? Where can you find the rich mix and independent choice that only the fine-grain of old cities seem to offer?

Where is the city that has its own identity and wears this identity as a badge of success – a city going places; a city willing to constantly evolve and therefore experiment with new concepts: an emerging place?

STABLE COMMUNITIES

In our ambition to build stable communities, have we had any better success? If we looked at any project we would see the standard headline ' a great place to bring up families' in blazing lights on its social development strategy. Once again, do we really understand the values and needs of 'stable communities, and can we really determine these? It certainly has not been in the mono-cultural one and two bedroom apartment living that has proliferated in our towns and cities in recent years, or the quasi-village lifestyles that the housebuilders have offered us.

> *A healthy social life is found only, when in the mirror of each soul the whole community finds its reflection, and when in the whole community the virtue of each one is living*

— Rudolf Steiner

Where are we making the great districts, neighbourhoods and quarters that 'stable communities' want to live in? The places where people can conform or express themselves as individuals? The street that Timmy can ride his bike down, where Nan can stroll to the local shop? Where are the choices that we can make throughout our lifetime: a long-life, loose-fit place? Where can we act as informed citizens?

How are we measuring the performance and health of our communities? This may seem like a strange question. After all, communities are organic and ever-evolving entities, right? Much of the research surrounding social and community problems in rapid growth communities has been based on objective indicators such as assessments of housing shortages, inadequate police forces and protection, the lack of medical care and facilities, and drug and alcohol abuse. Unfortunately, the use of these metrics tends to produce a limited view of possible social problems. Trying to benchmark and measure something as inherently chaotic and dynamic as community performance, health, or the new metrics thrown up by community collaboration can be extremely challenging.

Where are the intangibles: sense of community, social capital, well being, and happiness and where are metrics for them? The reality is that this type of data is now expected from neighbourhood managers and people who want a number to tell the whole story (mostly because they are not part of the community itself and it's really hard to explain the impact of a great community to an outsider). In the end, it comes down to defining social capital and this is incredibly elusive. It is measurable, but only relative to the source. After all, how do you measure happiness? Everyone has a different experience of it), which probably makes it the most perfectly decentralised system This is where we are headed, but so many people can't grasp that yet.

Given that these metrics are not just simple performance indicators to be measured by some bureaucrat in some dusty office, the real question lies in how we create the conditions for these and allow these intangibles to flourish.

SUSTAINABLE DEVELOPMENT

Finally, lets look at our successes in sustainable development. There is no shortage of efforts in the sustainability arena. Most of these efforts tend to be focused on either: LEARNING (developing knowledge), INFLUENCING (developing motivation in people and organisations), or DOING (developing skills and actually implementing things). Somehow all of these often well intended efforts don't add up to even the sum of their parts and analysis suggests that the main reasons for this are:

- Most efforts concentrate solely on social or economic or environmental agendas with few overlaps. Critically, we have not identified a single mechanism that effectively joins together learning, talking and doing.

- Many efforts are sector or discipline specific... driven by their niche interests... uninterested in broader sustainability goals. Some pursue short term technical fixes driven by narrow business perspectives.

- Many are driven by single-discipline professionals who are not trained or perhaps inclined to take a broad view.

- Some are think tanks burdened by dogma or driven by the need to achieve short-term political goals.

- Many are staffed by well meaning people with little relevant technical education who consequently find it very hard to get beyond the greenwash or green confusion to the substantive truth.

Many if not most of the challenges that we face arise from our approach to urban living. We have understood this for some time now and most of us would recognise these challenges. As such we find it surprising that there is very little urban theory that deals with the complex overlap of sustainability and urbanism.

Our urban design education has grown from a utopian townscape tradition and have not tackled the complexity of cities and large towns. Most courses have been grown from within a modernism and garden city tradition and are buried deep in the realms of planning or architecture. Most courses have tried to bolt on sustainability but have not been able to apply it in real life conditions. In reality, there is a disconnect between sustainability, change and urbanism in most courses. Even those teaching sustainability have failed to make the link that good urbanism should equal good sustainability. Moreover, we need to be able to move beyond single focus approaches. An excellent way of doing this would be through embracing the interface between urban design and urban living, cultural and business assets, political and social needs, financial drivers and value, innovation and creativity – a way where the 'Resilient City' meets the 'Talented City'.

Smart Urbanism provides a practical, relevant and useful unifying theme that will enable us to make progress towards meeting the challenges. It means taking professionals out of their silos and getting them to mix with the 'new normal' and the 'new local'.

THE PERFECT STORM

We often talk of paradigm shift but most often it is wishful thinking, us hoping that the weather will change for the better. Real shifts stall because interests are not aligned. The Haight-Ashbury movement of the 1960s pointed to a time where social and economic concerns were at a heightened state, the political concerns were not. The oil crisis of the 1970s gave us an opportunity to address the environmental concerns of the time. But instead of change, apathy happened!

In the same way we could have shifted our planning, design and delivery paradigms with the Urban Renaissance agenda of the early 2000s. We just ended up wasting a good word. Sustainability, not being dealt with seriously enough, is in danger of suffering a similar fate.

Apathy can be overcome by enthusiasm, and enthusiasm can only be aroused by two things: first, an ideal, which takes the imagination by storm, and second, a definite intelligible plan for carrying that ideal into practice.

—Arnold Toynbee

A perfect storm is an expression that describes an event where a rare combination of circumstances will aggravate a situation drastically. The term is also used to describe a hypothetical weather system that happens to hit at a region's most vulnerable area, resulting in the worst possible damage by an event of its magnitude. As such, the term is used by newsreaders to amplify a point, by environmentalist to drive home a concern or by economists to describe an unusual condition.

What we have now is the perfect storm. It is defined by the coming together of all the 'weather patterns' in heightened states of upheaval – economic, social, environmental and, to these, now add political. This is our rare combination that has hit us at our most vulnerable time. Apathy will not help. This is why we need to be thinking differently, imaginatively and with enthusiasm... together!

The theorem is not new. Schumacher, in his book 'Small is Beautiful', said it some years ago. He proposed the idea of "smallness within bigness": a specific form of decentralisation. He faulted conventional economic thinking for failing to consider the most appropriate scale for an activity, blasting notions that "bigger is better," and questioning the appropriateness of using mass production in developing countries, promoting instead "production by the masses." The proposition still has a safe haven in the EF Schumacher Society, an organisation to mobilise and inspire citizen-activists around his theories, all waiting for a time like this.

So, in our new decentralised, multiple interaction, bottom-up changing world, thinking MASSIVE SMALL is not just a good idea. In our perfect storm it is now an imperative.

Everyone has a plan
'til they get punched
in the mouth.

—Mike Tyson

BROKEN

'The old models are broken...', the words of Sir Bob Kerslake, formerly of the Homes and Community Agency. But are these models dead or just sleeping? Some would be inclined to blame the current recession for breaking these models. 'It will all get better', they say, 'when confidence returns'. Others would say the models were broken long before the recession. Did we really get it right before or were we just flogging a dead horse? Like Woolworths, they would say that the recession didn't kill the business; it merely buried it. So is this a time to reflect and change our approaches or is a paradigm shift upon us, whether we like it or not?

Lets get to the root of 'Broken'. If we understand where we are coming from we will better understand the nature and extent of this shift and therefore, where we need to go – our thinking, our tools and our fixes. So, lets look at the processes, practices and myths that dominate urban planning, design and delivery in more detail and see how it has an effect on development and, ultimately, urban life.

Success and failure of urban transformation processes cannot be measured by short-term growth alone. A booming economy with an over-inflated property market can banish all creative energy from the city, making it impossible for young and weak economies to thrive, potentially endangering what one might call a sustainable mix. Both scenarios reveal a crisis in current planning tools, which fail, to different degrees, to initiate and direct sustainable urban change.

While traditional state initiated planning is no longer affordable, the radical shift to neo-liberal planning policies fails to offer inclusive models that will lead to our competitive cities, our stable communities or our sustainable developments. Boom and gentrification can lead to social exclusion and an increasingly divided urban society, while the failure of market-driven development to adapt in the context of economic collapse has led to apathy and stagnation. Both wholesale renewal – the concern expressed so well in Owen Hatherly's book 'A Guide to the New Ruins of Great Britain' – and neglect are symptoms of a crisis, which should be considered as an opportunity to critically examine and question the existing planning, design and delivery procedures and consider alternative models of development.

Unsustainable location + overgrown airfield = Brownfield site
Brownfield site + Mixed Uses = Urban Village
Urban Village + Suburban Location = Sustainable Urban Extension
Sustainable Urban Extension + State Hype = Sustainable Community
Sustainable Community + Remote Unsustainable Location = Eco-Town

—Rob Cowan (Plandemonium, 2010)

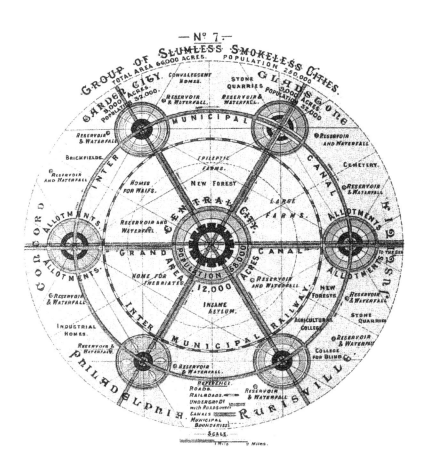

Le Corbusier's 'Contemporary City of Three Million Inhabitants' (1929) and
Ebenezer Howard's 'Social City' (1898): the roots of the anti-city movement.

ON URBAN PLANNING

Let's start with what we know:

- The planning system is not working for cities. We have a development control system, not a progressive enabling system. Planning, by its nature, is fundamentally reactive rather than proactive. When it does manage to take the initiative, it has to justify itself by creating special policy areas, as if to make clear that this is the exception, not the rule. Plans like this are out of date before they are written.

- The system is tortuously quasi-legal, doing its best to avoid any basis in physical design.

- It does not look to urban structure, except where a new road scheme is identified.

- It cannot deal with parts of a city beyond thinking of each part as a site.

- It cannot deal with the urban grain except through the application of design codes, which are more about development control than about creating an essential order and medium for the place to evolve.

- It fails to give a vision of a place except through words. A development plan 'map' does little more than define policy areas or constraints.

In truth, we are still using tools that work for our old industrial society, which tended to be monolithic and largely static. They are not fit for purpose in our multiple action, highly mobile, responsive post-industrial society. Here things have been happening despite our current tools not working. It is however on sustainability that the planning system is guilty of many of its superficial clichés. Just consider Rob Cowan's observation in Plandemonium on progress in planning over the past years.

When a political demagogue speaks of 'freedom' and 'justice', beware. Both are in danger, and in dank cellars those who dare challenge the new orthodoxy are having their fingernails slowly pulled out. When the planner speaks of sustainability, beware. This monstrously ill-defined, abstract concept is likely to be masking the incompetent application of some half-formed idea vaguely related to the use of resources. Freedom and justice are noble concepts and useful words. It is just that history teaches us not to accept them at face value. So too can sustainability be a useful concept, and the word can be called into service as a convenient chapter heading. But we are deluded if we believe that there is a simple thing called sustainability that, by merely invoking the word, can be made to infuse a planning policy or development concept with unchallengeable virtue.

The truth is the planning system has the wrong definers of success to guide positive change and many of the metrics we use are at odds with sustainable development. It is in our built environment that we can see the consequences of unchallenged market forces at work across all sectors: the edge-of-town centre foodstore, the formulaic housing development, the sterile business park and the 'nowhere' high street.

UNDERSTANDING REFORM

Our towns and cities, far from being expressions of regional identity and local response have become 'same-old, same-old' places, indistinguishable from one another – "bland identikit towns dominated by a few bloated retail behemoths" (New Economics Foundation, 2004). We use retail floorspace, defined through studies undertaken by vested-interest retail strategists, to define quantum of development in a town centre. The consequence is 347 foodstore applications (almost one per day) approved last year – the outcomes that fundamentally contradict the definition of localism.

The same applies to how we view housing, neighbourhoods, open space and employment land. Our metrics are wrong. Our values, ambitions and drivers of change are contradictory. We need reform but not at the expense of getting it wrong again.

In truth, the planning system cannot deal with complexity: so, it will be badly equipped to deal with the New Normal and the New Local. Like a user interface on a computer, the planning function sits on top of a flawed and outdated operating system. In recent years, what we know as urban design has been adapted as the friendly interface to the planning system. Although this has been a big step forward, it has disguised the true source of the problem. Further progress depends on changing the operating system.

The government has announced a fundamental reform of the planning system in England, but we have heard this before? In previous instances we just ended up changing words that just served to confuse further. In defence of the last round of changes, we were equipped with some of the necessary tools. We just failed to use them or have the confidence to apply them. Local Development Orders, which could have been used to guide and shape change in a progressive manner, were dismissed in favour of long, protracted Area Action Plans. Rather than the planning system giving certainty we have created uncertainty. We cannot afford to waste years in doing it all over again with the same outcomes. This reform must be more than shuffling deckchairs on the Titanic. It must use new thinking.

No matter what immediate changes are made to help the planning system work well, the problems lie deep in the anti-city origins of modern town planning, born of Ebenezer Howard's Garden Cities movement and the International Congress of Modern Architecture (CIAM) Charter of Athens. They are at the heart of the Town and Country Planning Act (no mention of city there). Cities have a wonderful ability to renew themselves – if we let them. For a hundred years we have handicapped them in our search for utopian forms, whether garden city or modernist.

> *We celebrate the good intentions of the two movements that in the twentieth century set about reshaping urban life. We mourn their faded dreams, and regret the malign influence they exert from beyond the grave. Both were anti-city.*
>
> — Re:Urbanism, 2002

INVESTING A NEW CONFIDENCE

With planning having lost confidence in its ability to get to grips with its physical dimension, mixed use has been adopted as the panacea. The new orthodoxy is to mix the uses up, regardless of context, and regardless of the interdependencies and viability of certain uses. Too often the result is not integrated, mixed-use places but isolated, mixed-use projects. As well as this, the preferred development control weapon of choice is now directed at 'form': what will it look like? Tall buildings strategies, building heights assessments, visual impact studies have replaced control of functions. 'Scale and character' are now loaded in both barrels.

Rather than being scared of physical planning because of previous failures, we need to invest a new confidence in the process: this time, rooted in a clear understanding about how cities work. The first step is to understand the overall structure of the city and its component parts – its localities [the district, quarter and neighbourhood] – and how they fit together. The second step is to understand the importance of the grain of the city that allows for a myriad of responses to emerge over time.

Run down areas and sites are automatically identified as 'zones of change', thus they are in the system – they get a status, demand investment and are prioritised. But do they automatically require fixing because they are run-down? In our striving for equity are we being fair to other places that will benefit from this investment? And, in our obsession with neatness, are we failing to recognise that many of these areas offer the first rung on the economic ladder for many new ventures? Perhaps turning a blind eye or managing their decline is often the best action.

Everyone is agreed: as much development as possible should be directed to sites that have been built on before – the brownfield sites. But as well as asking if a site has been used previously, we should be asking two further questions. Does this site have what it takes to become a successful urban place? If not, are we willing to invest in it sufficiently to create that potential? Beneath many brownfields is a greenfield waiting to get out. The disused airfield, the scene of many our professed 'eco-towns' is – let's face it – a field. The isolation hospital is isolated. No brownfield site is beyond reclamation and reuse – at a price. To often this price is bad urbanism.

But to make continuous, successful urbanism out of them needs something more than the run-of-the-mill skills of site development that are usually applied in such places. If our development policy is to improve on failure, we need some credible evidence that we are capable of creating the conditions for success this time round.

Planners will not prevent the city from flying but they may, by many of their actions, keep it in a continuous stall. This means that good things will continue to happen despite planning not because of it. Planning should now be enabling not restricting. It should be about defining the essential order, which fosters collective or individual response. It should be searching for the lightest touch not for the biggest stopping power!

That is, Modernism of the icon, of the city academies where each fundamentally alike yet bespoke design embodies a vacuous aspirationalism; a Modernism without politics, without the utopianism, or without any conception of the polis. Modernism as a shell.

—Owen Hatherly

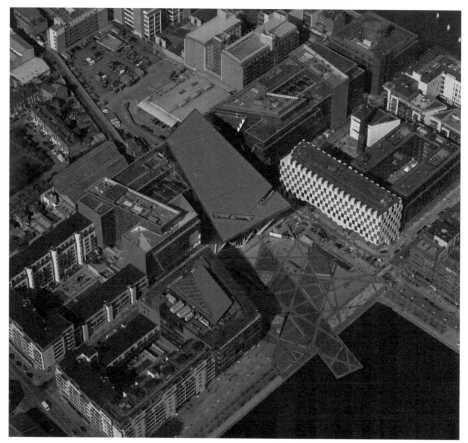

Grand Canal Docks, Dublin: Planning the extraordinary within an essential order (Urban Initiatives, 2010)

ON DESIGN

It is now well recognised that the modern city has proved unsatisfactory in application because it destroyed the elements of the city – street, block, the discrete public space and differentiated private place. But the underlying Modernist philosophy has not been displaced in proposals for urban redevelopment in Britain today. The thinking process accompanying this still results in the architectural objectification of urbanism; the design of cities continuing to be evaluated as a composition of distinct rational elements. Bradford, Barnsley, Manchester and many others have fallen to this curse. In reinstating the catalogue of urban elements, the city or neighbourhood block, for example, has been substituted for the "site" without any meaningful and critical re-evaluation of the spatial framework that must accompany it.

Even those analytical processes that are intended to rationally determine urban form are surprisingly anti-urban. Methodology still separates activities and uses, making each part more manageable and comprehensible for development packaging – the results lending themselves more to the interpretation of the architectural component than of complex urban elements. The functional programme as a determinant is invariably too inflexible because it fixes identities and relationships in precise building form thus limiting responsive action by restricting growth and change, alternatives and adaptation – the essential ingredients in a constantly evolving ecological process.

> *The attraction of form-based architecture is stronger today than ever with all major cities hosting buildings by the great modernists of our day. Many extraordinary, excellent designs follow the tradition of an ideal and specific form that solves a particular brief. Increasingly, though, the form and the brief are based on unapologetically personal rather than universal truths. So parts of our cities are becoming 'zoos' for exotic and delightful buildings; the more remarkable and varied the species contained, the more, somehow, each zoo comes to resemble other zoos and therefore comes to lose any sense of place.*

— Alex Lipschutz

In addition, modernism's prejudice against the existing city is implicitly retained. The alternative approach originally espoused by Jacobs, Bernard Rudofsky and now by a new brand of 'emergence' theorists is that the opposite should be the case. Cities and buildings need to be made of much more general, simple ingredients. Bottom up rather than top down.

Although the traditional city with its "real" streets, blocks and urban grain is vaguely advocated, it continues to be seen as a problem rather than a solution by many architects. We saw this in our work on the Grand Canal Docks masterplan in Dublin, where having developed a robust urban structure with streets, lots and blocks that easily accommodated the special architectural elements - Daniel Liebeskind's Grand Canal Theatre and the Martha Schwartz's public square - many architects regarded the urban design constraints as too limiting. They, of course, wanted everything to be special. Despite their protestations, the scheme has worked remarkably well and is only let down where the original rules were broken.

THE FAILURE OF DESIGN TO DELIVER

If our planning models have failed has success in design been any better? Let's examine three cases, the sustainable urban extension, the inner-city neighbourhood renewal project and the high-density mixed-use precinct; all expounded as urban design successes in recent years. All are examples of large-scale masterplans but what have they really achieved?

Most sustainable urban extensions are merely by-pass infill based on a spurious notion of a walkable neighbourhood but with nothing meaningful to walk to – often merely a reworking of the old design models but with 'axes'. They desperately cling onto existing settlements like a baby monkey on its mother's back rather than rooting themselves into the urban fabric. For the private sector, dealing with the adjacent community is too difficult, so places revert to being archipelagos of suburbia, justified on environmental grounds, but still just propagating sprawl, albeit at a higher density than previously built. So what makes them sustainable?

Park Central in Birmingham is a much applauded inner city renewal scheme, reaping all the awards in recent years. It would tick every box in urban design best practice. It is well designed and executed. It is also devoid of soul. Where we have moved to even higher densities, seen as the prerequisite for urban life, we have also failed. This is a pattern in many of our recent developments. What we have in return is a kind of 'Starbucks urbanism' – superficial and transient. Nothing like the qualities we have in the successful urban places that we value.

Despite employing the best designers, having all the right conditions to deliver design quality and being supported by good clients, many masterplans have failed to achieve urbanity – surely the only real measure of success. High design, despite all of the Commission for Architecture and the Built Environment's efforts, has not given us what we expected.

> *Too often the issues are presented as a battle of architectural styles. Take your choice: the new-urbanist, traditional urbanism of Leon Krier; or the modernist, post-urbanism of Rem Koolhaas. That false polarity neatly diverts the discussion up a fetid cul-de-sac of architectural introspection. Enthusiastic coteries join their heroes at the extremes, in glorious isolation from any possible collective view of the future of cities.*

— Re:Urbanism, 2002

Successful cities have a coherence above and beyond the individual expression of particular buildings. The special is complemented by the ordinary, the city's essential fabric. Some of the best new urban architecture, particularly in Ireland and Scotland, is reinventing the traditions of the terrace and the tenement. Designers in the modern idiom are inspired, not intimidated, by the past: it just makes good sense. Architects may complain that the constraints of urbanism compromise their artistic integrity. So why is it that the best designers perform so brilliantly when the brief sets particularly challenging constraints?

The last time we saw radical architecture was in the 60s and 70s: a time of architecture without architects, community architecture, self-help, all challenging the role of the designer. Since then, architecture in this country has retreated from any overt political or social agenda. Instead of being radical in any real sense, the most it can be is 'avant garde'. Formal, technological and stylistic inventions are its only innovations. Subsumed to marketing and branding, architecture offers only novelty rather than any challenge to the status quo or any alternatives for change. The shock of the new has been replaced by the consumption of the new because architecture has now become fully assimilated into the society of the spectacular.

However, the architectural establishment in practice and academia cannot see the irony of all this. The fact that anything so stylistically regressive might be considered radical is beyond their comprehension. Here we see another, hidden, unchallenged 'truth' – that architecture has become obsessed with product. Only innovation of the product is legitimised. Radical approaches, radical reframing of professional roles is ignored. In part, this is to do with architecture's anachronistic idea of the architect as the romanticised model of the artist. This is the fictional realm of Ayn Rand's 'Fountainhead' – a million miles from the 21st Century reality of building production. But this fantasy is more damaging than the mere self-delusion of an entire profession. The artist model is damaging architecture – and by extension, urbanism. It focuses on the product and presents it as creative signature of a single intelligence and will. The coherence of the object is the single concern and success measured in large part by the degree to which a singular artistic vision has been pushed through despite the possibility of other, conflicting concerns.

At the urban scale, design cannot be the singular vision of a lone artist. Cities are constituted from complex and diverse human interactions. Cities are where potential for conflict must be resolved and much of their creative energy flows from this fact. The design of cities therefore cannot be based on an architectural approach extended to the city scale. We must think of cities in a different time-frame from architecture: centuries rather than decades. The structures of the city must survive independently of its buildings. 'Big architecture' imposes an architectural time-frame on the urban structure, frustrating the city's potential to develop the kind of emergent, higher-order behaviour that Jane Jacobs celebrated. Living cities bubble like pots of porridge. Who knows where the next bubble will burst?

> *A good urban design solution can rescue a bad building, but a great building will rarely rescue poor urban design.*
>
> — Paul Finch

Contrary to the impression given by the master plan, the aim of planning is not to visualise – and then to achieve – a permanent end state. Every place is always changing, either for the better or for the worse. Unless we accept that fact, we will succeed neither in managing decline in the places where that is appropriate, nor in supporting success in the places where there is the most potential for that.

Like Daleks we chant the mantra of 'Outputs! Outputs! Outputs!' Investment at all costs has often meant just that: bad urbanism.

—Re:urbanism 2002

ON DELIVERY

Einstein's famous quote, 'Insanity is doing the same thing over and over again... expecting different results', seems real now. Most large masterplans have not delivered in this country. Despite urban design being at the forefront of the current agenda in the past decades, you can probably count the number of implemented schemes on your hand. The reason is simple. We have tried to replace the role of the public sector with the private sector and in doing so we have limited the true potential of the private sector to operate effectively at all levels.

We have also created a contorted procurement process that ensures that we get exactly the wrong outcome we. Steve Tolson in his paper 'The Regeneration Crisis' says that the average competitive dialogue process costs the same as building 75 houses or one primary school. Philip Howard in the 'Death of Common Sense' says that in America one third of the capital cost of a project is spent on procurement. With so much focus on reducing risk, the biggest risk is nothing happening.

The private sector can deliver a successful product but struggles to deliver a successful place. That can only be the role of those who have a long-term view of a place. Horizons are too far for the private sector unless they are operating as a 'quasi-estate'. The public sector is expecting the private sector to deliver projects that are too big, too intertwined and often too self-centred – the 'single saviour' approach. You know, stick all your problems in the problem basket and get the private sector to sort it out. This will get the public sector off the hook and solve all the problems of a place, they think. Wrong! Otherwise, why would so many big projects still be struggling after all these years, kept alive on the defibrillator of hope and expectation?

BIGNESS

All of the case studies talked about in the previous chapter – the sustainable urban extension, the inner-city neighbourhood renewal project and the high-density mixed-use precinct – have common denominators. They all have single formulaic offers, all with a single hand and all delivered by means of a single approach. All start with the large site and move straight to the scheme with nothing between. They are like large problem mountains that only become resolved when the climb has reached the apex. Only then, you still need the energy to get down from the top and this is where most schemes falter.

Large sites need to be broken down into problem hills or, better still, many problem bumps. But many developers like keeping their options open and one scheme merely replaces another as ownership, markets and competition forces change. Why else have so many places had so many masterplans?

Why is it that the machinery of regeneration and development is directed so emphatically to site assembly? Are we so convinced that putting more land into the control of fewer people is always a good thing?

Big buildings need big floorplates but this does not warrant the sheer scale of the effort in many places – the loss of finer grain of ownership, management, design and variety that so damages our cities. It changes historic patterns of use and ownership just as much as a tall building might, yet it is somehow seen as more acceptable to spread large buildings across an entire city block rather than let a building rise higher from a smaller footprint. Temple Bar in Dublin shows how the cumulative effect of countless small carefully designed interventions adds up to a far bigger picture than any single solution.

Consolidation sterilises entire city blocks rendering them less capable of responding to changes in markets or technology and requiring bigger, more costly, more dramatic intervention to change in the future. It curtails movement, the permeability of the city that might otherwise offer choice of routes and encourage us to wander in the city confident that if we explore an unknown route we can easily find our way back. It creates a megastructure that distorts development and movement as well as long-term influences on city development that is disproportionate to its physical size.

The recent debacle over London's Elephant and Castle is as good an example as any. The 1960s-built megastructure had failed. When megastructures fail, they fail disastrously. The council's proposed solution: replace it with an even larger megastructure. This one would have a level of complexity that depended on everything significant happening together, rather than taking an incremental, fine-grain approach. After years of preparatory work, the plan unravelled. Only the public sector can deliver a project of this scale by becoming the development 'parceller', opening up the opportunities to a much wider group of players.

We need to discover the lost art of subdivision. Areas where significant change is expected, and large sites are due for development, should be planned by the public sector as integrated extensions or repairs of the city's physical fabric. Such a planning framework will treat those areas and sites as parts of the town or city, not stand-alone sites, allowing them to be developed in smaller increments than is usual.

> *Incrementalism is central to the future of development. This way of thinking about the world works with the grain of society rather than posting top-down technocratic solutions...(sic) small scale strategies and initiatives, if there are enough of them, can become a very big idea indeed.*

— Paul Finch (Architect's Journal) 9th December 2010

How thinking has changed! Gone are the days where big architecture will save us. Bigness has been a recurring theme in many urban projects in the recent past: big sites that need big solutions; and big buildings that need big developers. Our fascination lies in their sheer scale and bravado, in their ambition and in their failure. These are the projects that hold cities and towns to ransom. They are 'category killers' by the monopolising effect they have in the market, either real or by their promise. In their bigness they prevent positive things happening at a smaller scale.

They are the fire that sucks the oxygen out of the room. None, more so, than the large sites on the outskirts of many of our towns and villages that have been optioned by the housebuilders with the view to meeting old growth targets. Vast areas have been consented but things are not moving. Whatever the reason, market conditions or not, they are the agents against bottom-up change and something has to be done to come up with better practices to avoid both strategic landbanking and mitigate the extreme damping effect they have on the market. At the same time we need to keep up the steady flow of better housing. If there is one model that is fundamentally broken it is the volume housebuilding market. Surely we now know that gigantism is the final throw by a desperate gambler who has tried everything else?

An inability to see beyond the big picture can create a proposal for a development scheme that only a handful of major developers are capable of delivering. The result is that such projects rarely happen. Often they are delayed to the next economic cycle. Occasionally a major project slips through, but the rest are doomed to endless redesign. Yet still too many of those who instigate and fund development feel at ease only if they can draw a firm red line round a large development site. Bigness hasn't worked here.

Big sites should not, however, be confused with 'big pictures'. Every place needs a big picture to guide its future growth and change, but big pictures need big walls. Successful cities and towns create the 'galleries' for these big pictures – their own city or town plans. Big pictures can take two forms. The first: Big picture as big splashes on the canvas – a Pollock or a Calder. It lives when the splash is made and then subsides. Some call it 'big' architecture, the iconic masterplan or perfect building that will save us – also called the quick fix, the 'wow factor' or the Bilbao effect.

The second type: Big picture as the million dabs on the canvas. Nobody can deny that Monet's 'Water lilies' is a great big picture. It is the result of an infinite number of transactions on the canvas. It only comes to life when the last dab is made and then it is timeless. Of course, cities continue to make new dabs or freshen old ones, but this type of big picture is invested with a stronger relationship with its viewer. It is more than iconic, it is a masterpiece!

We now need an upside down version of the 'Big Architecture' approach propagated in the last decade. This has been the underlying fault in many of our masterplans in recent years – the hit and miss of the 'wow-factor'. Many of these have forced the architecture rather than facilitating it – plans that are too predisposed to produce single outcomes rather than offering individual responses. The fault of the masterplanner lies in not understanding the absolute need for complexity and an obsession with making the plan look 'interesting'. In the world of 'Form Follows Function', if the building doesn't work we need to go back to reworking the masterplan. And so it goes!

Our job as urban designers must be to create the conditions for the 'million dabs' to occur – or, expressed differently, create the fertile fields for new emergent behaviours. We must make a city of a thousand designers.

The world will not evolve past its current state of crisis by using the same thinking that created the situation.

—Albert Einstein

THINKING

Cities are victims of outdated thinking. Narrow reductionism thought processes linger under the influence of the pseudo-sciences, drawing from past philosophies that have little relevance today. It follows from Einstein's view that a new reductionist set of theories will not solve our problems.

Every theory claims its own truths, even if it is not very different from last year's theory. Indoctrinated by the scientific method, we pose hypotheses, analyse, apply our new theories, and synthesise. The truth provides an unshakeable basis for practice. Until the next theory comes along. We cannot therefore follow this traditional scientific model or, in our world, the predict-and-provide approach to shaping our fixes. The idea that we can deal with complexity by setting different trajectories to catch up or influence physical outcomes in cities has never worked. As soon as we implement a new fix it is out of date.

It's quite obvious that political systems thrive on their polarities – regulation versus deregulation; libertarianism versus paternalism; big government versus big society (centralism versus localism); and so on. Quite often, in the feverish pursuit of change, politicians tend to 'throw the baby out with the bathwater' and we lose some of the best things. The last government's reform to the planning system amounted to tinkering with the mechanics rather than facing up to the need for fundamental change.

The real risk in the recent announcements by the UK government is that 'fundamental reform of the planning system' just becomes a different way of using the same old thinking. We need reform but further progress depends on fundamentally changing the operating system. Like Apple we need to 'Think Different' but, like them, our mantra should be 'Evolution not Revolution'. Small changes can make enormous differences.

Like any emergent system, a city is a pattern in time. Dozens of generations come and go, conquerors rise and fall, the printing press appears, then the steam engine, then radio, television, the Web – and beneath all that turbulence, a pattern retains its shape.

—Steven Johnson, "Emergence"

THE OBSESSION WITH CERTAINTY

Rationalism, that bright dream of figuring out everything in advance and setting it forth precisely in a centralised regulatory system, has made us blind. Obsessed with certainty, we see almost nothing.

    —Philip Howard 'The Death of Common Sense'

In recent years, 'form' has merely taken the place of 'function' as a determinant in a continuing partial approach to the problem. Little is offered in the way of providing a robust and adaptable model of city building, capable of guiding growth and change in such a way that the preconditions for high quality environments are optimised at the outset.

Environments of this quality cannot be created by the unthinking application of limiting rules or theories that only dictate end state conditions. The 'one-size-fits-all' approach has never worked for us. This does not mean that we need no rules or theories. We still need complex choices to be structured but these must still allow for infinite possibilities.

A 'flexible approach' to planning is now constantly referred to as a solution to the planning dilemma. "Planning gets in the way!" - those in power say, but other than offering a diluted laissez-faire response to market forces, the underlying need for certainty is still a fundamental driver of our industry. Not only are we obsessed with the need for certainty but also we want to know what it will be like in twenty years. We try to quantify uses without really having any understanding of future demands. We use sophisticated models to predict outcomes, knowing we have no faith in them. We show visions of how they will look without believing in them. In reality we should be asking the question, "What gives us enough certainty and enough possibility?" Then let's determine how we move forward.

So, it follows that in addition to 'command-and-control', 'predict-and-provide' also does not work. Taking this into account, what is now required is a new all-embracing view about urbanity and its potentials, and the application of those ideas which release these potentials and which free the creative ingenuity of man. In adopting a holistic view of the city, one recognises the necessary complexity of man, his life, and the role of the environment in his life; which recognises too the complex processes of interdependence and reinforcement that constitute the essence of urbanity. This view requires an understanding that does not imply that we know everything about man and his environment, but rather what should be left to the ingenuity of the individual and what should be provided to stimulate that ingenuity to achieve better places.

We also need to recognise that 'bottom-up' systems don't work without some form of 'top-down'. The real question, in thinking differently, is what type of behaviour we need in these 'top-down' systems? Whilst this chapter is not intended to be a treatise on complexity, it does look to show how we can learn from its principles and processes in applying it to our new bottom-up world.

IT'S NOT THAT WE THINK, IT'S HOW WE THINK!

In defining the term 'complexity', theorists often refer to systems that are composed of many parts. It is certainly true that complexity usually arises when a system consists of many interconnected parts. However, the number of parts is not an absolute guide. Large systems are sometimes very simple in their structure and behaviour. On the other hand, some systems with very simple structure behave in very complicated and unpredictable ways.

> COMPLEXITY *The state of being composed of many interconnected parts. In a complex system a large number of independent elements interact. The system acquires collective properties of its own – a life of its own, you might say – through those elements clashing with or accommodating each other. As the system becomes more complex, new collective properties emerge and new ways of understanding them need to be found. Small events can result in unexpectedly large changes. It is the structure of the networks that we must understand, not their details. The structures can be understood only as being constantly in transition as they respond to ever-changing conditions. Influencing complex systems is a matter of managing change, not of achieving equilibrium. A system in equilibrium is one in which its elements have ceased to interact. Apart from somewhere like Pompey, that is a condition not found in cities. Much of the least successful town planning and urban design is a consequence of visualising a condition of equilibrium and trying to achieve it. The drawings may be impressive, but they will never be realised.*

—Rob Cowan, The Dictionary of Urbanism

Complexity denotes phenomena that are difficult to describe, understand, or control. However, being difficult to understand is not sufficient for something to be complex. It is only when the difficulty arises from richness in structure or behaviour that a thing is considered complex. Complexity is often defined in negative fashion. Things are deemed complex by virtue of not being simple. For instance, a system is complex if it is not tractable by standard methods of analysis. Likewise, a system is complex if the behaviour of individual elements cannot be understood by studying them in isolation.

Finally, a system can be considered complex if it cannot be represented by a single model, but needs several different models, each representing different facets of the system, or different levels of abstraction. Complexity is probably best described as richness and variety, either in structure, or in the behaviour of a system.

> *Cities [are] problems in organized complexity, like the life sciences... city areas with flourishing diversity sprout strange and unpredictable uses and peculiar scenes. But this is not a drawback of diversity. This is the point ... of it.*

—Jane Jacobs

A classic exposition of the implications of the phenomenon of 'organised complexity' for city planners and urban designers was made by Jane Jacobs in her landmark book 'The Death and Life of Great American Cities' (1961). It is difficult to overstate its influence on the planning discipline in general, and on subsequent thinking about process and generativity in particular. When you are looking for a great quote, the great old lady is always there to oblige. In talking about 'The kind of problem a city is', Jacobs lucidly analysed the implications of the scientific advancements that were then occurring – in particular, the understanding of complex systems in which a number of factors were interrelated into an organic whole. This was important for urbanists because they needed to be sure they were thinking about the right kind of problem, and using the right tools to solve it.

As Jacobs would agree, the city is a 'superorganism', displaying properties of complexity well beyond the sum of its parts. That is why we cannot model cities using simple tools. It operates despite planning not because of it. Johnson sees the neighbourhood system of the city functioning as a kind of user interface for the same reason that traditional computer interfaces do: there are limits to how much complexity our brains can handle at any given time. We need visual interfaces on our desktop computers because the sheer quantity of information stored on our hard drives greatly exceeds the carrying capacity of the human mind.

Self-organising clusters of districts, neighbourhoods and quarters serve to make cities and towns more intelligible to the individuals who inhabit them and, as the building blocks of the city, can be influenced at many levels.

Complexity is a word that has frequently appeared in critical accounts of metropolitan space, but there are really two kinds of complexity fundamental to the city, two experiences with very different implications for the individuals trying to make sense of them. There is, first, the more conventional sense of complexity as sensory overload, the city stretching the human nervous system to its very extremes, and in the process teaching it a new series of reflexes – and leading the way for a complementary series of aesthetic values which develop out like a scab around the original wound. But complexity is not solely a matter of sensory overload. There is also the sense of complexity as a self-organising system. This sort of complexity lives up one level: it describes the system of the city itself, and not its experiential reception by the city dweller. The city is complex because it overwhelms, yes, but also because it has a coherent personality, a personality that self-organises out of millions of individual decisions, a global order built out of local interactions.

—Steven Johnson, Emergence

SELF-ORGANISING SYSTEMS

A lot has been written in recent years about emergence. Some regard it as a pseudo-science, a kind of hippy invention to tear down the walls of the establishment's reductionist ivory towers. Certainly, evidence shows that many articles have been written which start well but, challenged with showing how emergence can be applied, dissolve into soft, fuzzy focus and dodgy architectural constructs. Some have even said that emergence undermines the meaning and agenda of the science of complexity, which is a real science. They are probably right, we have been so caught up in the metaphors and psychedelia of the fractal geometries, the kaleidoscopic patterns and the sinister slime moulds that characterise emergence that we cannot see its true worth in influencing how we think of cities and their districts, neighbourhoods and quarters. We are wasting a good science. Mathieu Helie's Emergent Urbanism Network at the University of Montreal goes some way to addressing these misgivings, but is still mildly guilty of harking back to the superficial parts of emergent thinking's seventies' roots.

Others have used emergent thinking in urban design theory to meaningfully explain unintended consequences and novel patterns of city growth and neighbourhood formation but much of this lies in the academic cyberspace. For many theorists, such as Christopher Alexander, it has been used to explain the evolution of spontaneous settlements in third world conditions, to good effect.

Whatever the perspective, the fact remains that not much has been written about the application of emergence in the first world, other than regards historical processes. This does not mean that emergence is not relevant to the first world. Its scarcity is most likely due to the fact that the first world has had the most evolved top-down systems of control which has prevented any form of emergence. There was no audience. Localism opens up the potential to change this.

Emergent systems can be good innovators, and it is now well recognised that they tend to be more adaptable to sudden change than our more rigid hierarchical models. These qualities make the possibilities of bottom-up intelligence tantalising for towns and cities struggling to keep up with rapid change. Bottom-up systems lend themselves to adaptive self-organisation and we can learn from a number of sources where this has been effective – from cities and nature to the Web.

But emergent systems also display distinctly opposite outcomes. On the one hand they give rise to 'perpetual' or 'radical novelty', a property that displays new features not previously observed. This makes sense – if you allow for individual response, prepare to be surprised. On the other hand something else arises that totally contradicts what might be expected from this freedom of expression – that of 'regularity', a property characterised as having persistent, recurring structures, patterns and themes.

This contradiction could be explained in informal squatter settlements where, despite having the freedom to build what you want, people build remarkably similar things in conventional ways. In fact many squatter settlements display a dominance of regularities. So in emergent systems, freedom is not freely taken.

Another important contradiction and consequence of emergence is the tendency of individuals to group into hierarchical organisations. John Holland, in his book Emergence: From Chaos to Order, cites this as one of the important conditions needed to foster emergence. Hierarchies are common in complex systems. They usually arise either from the organisation of systems on different scales (for example in communities) or from interactions that impose order on the agents that comprise a system.

Hierarchies ensure total connectivity, but limit interactions (and hence complexity) between links up and down the hierarchy. So, in urban design this means that hierarchical spatial structures and networks are preconditions to organic growth and change.

WHAT IS COMPLEXITY SCIENCE?

Complexity is a real science precisely because it has developed new methods for studying regularities and not because it is a new approach for studying the complexity of the world.

—Steven Phelan, What is Complexity Science, really?

Science has always been about reducing the complexity of the world to (predictable) regularities. To a layperson, the behaviour of crowds is complex and chaotic, but Keith Still's work at Crowd Dynamics reduces that complexity to manageable regularities. The focus should be on the methods used to search for regularities. Complexity science introduces a new way to study regularities that differs from traditional science.

Traditional science has tended to focus on simple cause-effect relationships. Complexity science posits simple causes for complex effects. At the core of complexity science is the assumption that complexity in the world arises from simple rules. However, these rules (which are termed 'generative rules') are unlike the rules (or laws) of traditional science. Generative rules typically determine how a set of agents will behave in their virtual environment over time, including the interaction with other agents.

Unlike traditional science, generative rules do not predict an outcome for every state of the world. Instead, generative rules use feedback and learning to enable us to adapt to our environment over time. The application of these generative rules to a large population leads to emergent behaviour that may bear some resemblance to real world phenomena. Finding a set of generative rules that can mimic real world behaviour may help scientists predict, control, or explain hitherto unfathomable systems (such as cities and their districts, neighbourhoods and quarters).

The challenge for complexity science is to calibrate the computer models to real-world data. For instance, does the city or neighbourhood exhibit chaotic behaviour that can be mapped onto a simple equation. It is not too difficult to see that, from the historicist perspective, complexity science represents a good example of a developing applied research programs into city dynamics, smart grids or neighbourhood formation.

Urbanists and software designers have been experimenting with models that can simulate the ways that cities self-organise themselves over time. While actual cities are heavily shaped by top-down forces, such as planning policy and planning committees, we have long recognised that bottom-up forces play a critical role in city formation, creating distinct neighbourhoods and other unplanned demographic clusters. In recent years, some theorists have developed more precise models that re-create the neighbourhood-formation process with some precision.

The same can be said about many complex systems, from beehives and flocks of birds to the economy and the Internet. Whenever you have a multitude of individuals interacting with one another, there often comes a moment when disorder gives way to order and something new emerges: a pattern, a decision, a structure, or a change in strategy. It is from this controlled messiness that the wisdom of the collective emerges.

Steven Johnson's book 'Emergence' describes adaptive self-organising systems – systems that are made up of many interacting agents getting on with their lives who have no part in some overall plan, but who collectively come up with intelligent higher-level behaviour. An ant colony is a great example of this kind of system: nobody is technically "in charge", and yet somehow the ants manage to behave in astonishingly complex ways: shifting roles among the colony members in response to changing needs. It turns out that the world is filled with these systems, nowhere more so than in the formation of city districts, neighbourhoods and quarters.

In Johnson's view, the simplest rule of all the systems is 'learn from your neighbours'. A community in the game SimCity decides to lower its crime rate or pollution levels based on the crime or pollution in neighbouring blocks. All of these systems follow relatively simple rules, but they project those rules out over thousands (or, in the case of the brain, billions) of interacting agents. Given enough interactions, and given the right simple rules, something magical happens: the simulated city comes to life on the screen.

The study of emergence and complexity has helped businesses solve problems from optimising telecommunications links to loading and unloading airplanes to reducing traffic jams in major cities. It is impossible to understand tragedies from stampedes in busy stadiums to economic collapse without it. Peter Miller in his book, 'The Smart Swarm', gives a fascinating new take on the concept of collective intelligence and its colourful manifestations in some of our most complex problems. Looking at the ancient instincts of swarms gives us a compelling new understanding in solving complex business, politics, and technology problems.

Miller has identified four basic principles for self-organisation:

- The first principle of a smart swarm is self-organisation. Through the basic mechanisms of decentralised control, distributed problem solving and multiple interactions, members of a group without being told can transform simple rules of thumb into meaningful patterns of collective behaviour.

- The second principle of a smart swarm is 'diversity of knowledge' – which is basically achieved through a broad sampling of the swarm's options, followed by a friendly competition of ideas. Then using an effective mechanism to narrow down the choices, swarms can achieve 'wisdom of crowds' – and Miller shows how communities can build trust and make better decisions by adapting this principle.

- The third principle is indirect collaboration. If individuals in a group are prompted to make small changes to a shared structure that inspires others to improve it even further, the structure becomes an active player in the creative process. This is characterised in our Internet world through Wikis.

- The fourth principle is adaptive mimicking. With the example of flight behaviour of starlings, Miller shows how the basic mechanisms of coordination, communication and copying can unleash powerful waves of energy or awareness that race across a population evoking a feeling of mental telepathy.

We can also learn from the behaviour of complex systems in economics. The Santa Fe Institute defines six features:

A **Dispersed Interaction.** What happens in the economy is determined by the interaction of many dispersed, possibly heterogeneous, agents acting in parallel. The action of any given agent depends upon the anticipated actions of a limited number of other agents and on the aggregate state these agents co-create.

B **Mediated controls.** No global entity controls interactions. Instead, controls are provided by mechanisms of competition and coordination between agents. Economic actions are mediated by legal institutions, assigned roles, and shifting associations. Nor is there a universal competitor – a single agent that can exploit all opportunities in the economy.

C **Cross-cutting Hierarchical Organisation.** The economy has many levels of organisation and interaction. Units at any given level of behaviours, actions, strategies or products typically serve as "building blocks" for constructing units at the next higher level. The overall organisation is more than hierarchical, with many sorts of tangling interactions (associations, channels of communication) across levels.

D **Continual Adaptation.** Behaviours, actions, strategies, and products are revised continually as the individual agents accumulate experience – the system constantly adapts.

E **Perpetual Novelty.** These are continually created by new markets, new technologies, new behaviours, and new institutions. The very act of filling a niche may provide new niches. The result is ongoing, perpetual novelty.

F **Out-of-Equilibrium Dynamics.** Because new niches, new potentials, new possibilities, are continually created, the economy operates far from any optimum or global equilibrium. Improvements are always possible and indeed occur regularly.

THINKING

Taken together, these mechanisms explain how members of a group can transform simple rules into meaningful patterns of collective behaviour and give us some important lessons for the Localism agenda.

The greatest practical problem in dealing with complexity is how to analyse, interpret and manage real systems. Complexity theory does provide some sobering lessons that planners need to heed. One lesson is that complex processes are often inherently unpredictable. This makes it difficult to predict the precise effects of many planning strategies. Moreover, unexpected events become highly likely. It also means that the world can no longer afford ad hoc approaches to planning and development. Decision-making depends on reliable information. So the provision of timely, accurate and relevant information is one of the prime concerns.

Traditional methods of analysis and interpretation do not work for complex systems. The need to understand and manage complex systems has led to many active areas of research that attempt to devise methods for dealing with them. These new methods constitute entire new paradigms. An important part of this process is using effective mechanisms to narrow choices, something evolved societies have always done. Without a limiting of choice, self-organisation stalls.

THE PARADOX OF CHOICE

Are flexibility and choice, when used together, the two most dangerous words in the English language? Barry Schwarz in his book, 'The Paradox of Choice', has some interesting observations. As choice increases the exercising of choice diminishes and with this comes the fear of choice. In other words, have I made the right choice? He likens this to buying an insurance policy. As insurance companies offered more choice of complex products, prospective customers put off making any choice with the fear that they would make the wrong decision. As choice increased, take up reduced. Absolute choice was therefore no choice. What we are really looking for is limited choice with infinite possibilities... like a well-cooked meal that we can flavour! In urban terms this is what society has always done. Some call it vernacular, others refer to it as the prevailing norm: the rules in which urbanism can flourish at every level.

Choice architecture describes the way in which decisions are influenced by how the choices are presented, and is a term used by Cass Sunstein and economist Richard Thaler in the 2008 book 'Nudge: Improving Decisions about Health, Wealth, and Happiness'. They stress the importance of structuring complex choices and show that people adapt different strategies for making choices depending on the size and complexity of the available options: "When we face a small number of well-understood alternatives, we tend to examine all the attributes of all the alternatives and then make trade-offs when necessary. But when the choice set gets too large, we must use alternative (simplifying) strategies and these get us into trouble." Using choice architecture we can construct default choices and incentives to influence choice and this can be applied to the design of urban environments.

LEARNING FROM CROWDS

A Wiki was originally described as "the simplest online database that could possibly work." But, Wiki systems have shown that the simple freedom to create does not necessarily produce networks unless there also exists a simple interface to this network. Wiki systems also need simple rules.

The Wikipedia system catalysed the distributed knowledge of millions of people into an exponentially growing and internally coherent system – called "crowdsourcing." Translating crowdsourcing principles to planning processes, Christopher Alexander described in his book, 'The Oregon Experiment' how an institution could directly support the spontaneous development of its city or town.

There are a number of urban theorists who believe that a return to the type of spontaneous city growth that we experienced in historic settlements or that we currently experience in new squatter settlements is absolutely necessary for sustainability. Why do we not just sit back and let humans self-organise? Why have any rules?

However, even the most optimistic champions of self-organisation feel a little wary about the lack of control in such a process. Besides, we are not ants or bees or flocks of birds. We are more highly evolved, aren't we? But, understanding emergence has always been about giving up control, letting the system govern itself as much as possible, letting it learn from its actions. Others will argue that if techniques to produce a 'new essential order' are reintroduced that respect this condition, order will emerge out of the random actions of large numbers of individuals. With this insight, urban design is explained as the selection of effective urban growth processes that give rise to desirable patterns of urbanism. The real problem in much of this thinking is how we use it to shape well-established current processes of planning, design and delivery, in particular, in our developed countries – processes that place enormous emphasis on land value, speculation and obsession with neatness and control.

As always, building emergent systems doesn't guarantee that they will turn out to be better than the old solutions. To succeed you need to get the variables right.

VENUS AND MARS

A 'New Theory of Urban Design' (Christopher Alexander, 1987) amounted to a gauntlet thrown down to conventional urban design, not unlike that thrown down by Jane Jacobs three decades years earlier. Alexander himself was tentative about the particular methodology he proposed. Indeed he later offered his own critique of its shortcomings. But he was not then, nor has he been since, tentative about the key theoretical points on which this methodology differed from conventional practice:

- Urban design must not be an act of tabula rasa imposition of a form designed remotely, based upon an abstract program. It must understand, respect, and seek to improve the existing conditions.

- Urban design must incorporate the decisions and needs of the local stakeholders, as a matter not only of fairness, but also of the intrinsic quality of the result.

- Above all, urban design must be a generative process, from which a form will emerge – one that cannot be pre-planned or standardised, but will of necessity be, at least in some key respects, local and unique.

Michael Mehaffy, writing in the Journal of Urbanism, on 'Generative Methods in Urban Design' raises an important but significant difference between Christopher Alexander and the New Urbanist movement. Mehaffy's insight and writing is so good, it is not worth editing and is rather paraphrased below.

> The most notable example of an effort to implement Alexander's ideas – and Jacobs's in equal measure, it should be added – has been the New Urbanism movement. In his words, this is 'a highly effective organisation that propagated the modernist movement in architecture, which accelerated the kind of segregation and top-down formalism in city-planning that both Jacobs and Alexander decried'.

> By contrast, the New Urbanism is explicitly about mixed use, and, its proponents would argue, about process. For Alexander, however, the process is a laudable effort at reform that is still woefully inadequate for the challenge. Most importantly for Alexander, the process builds structures that are not at all generative, but based upon standardised templates, with the result that they feel lifeless and unsuccessful. They may have the outward appearance of a more organic neighbourhood, but they are, in the end, standardised reproductions.

> For Andres Duany, the figurehead for the New Urbanists, Alexander's critique misses a key point. Yes, there are standardised templates within The New Urbanism – as, for example, a basic plan drawing of the scheme. But that structure can then be adapted and allowed to serve as a skeletal form for more organic growth. In effect, it can serve as a kind of well-designed "trellis" on which organic growth can self-organise. Duany notes that such combinations of the standard and the contextual are common in nature.

Duany and others point to Alexander's own patterns as typological structures that are, in part, standardised elements within his own design system (though a networked one, and not a strict hierarchy). They are then adapted to the specific context, and used in a kind of flexible grammar. Duany believes he is doing something very similar (and indeed, often using Alexander's own patterns). "I am the best Alexandrian," he recently told the author.

Moreover, Duany believes Alexander is failing to come to terms with a core reality of modern technological society: that large numbers demand top-down management methods. In a mass society, the norm quickly reverts to chaos and kitsch. In order to implement Alexander's methods, this demands expert, top-down leaders for the design and construction process. For the New Urbanists, Alexander's proposal is to return to a painstaking one-off process of organic design, which is simply not up to the scale of the present challenge. Rather, we must create more automatic processes that generate the same result, not unlike seeds that generate vast numbers of living structures.

So Duany and other New Urbanists have turned to a new project: the development of codes that replace the old, destructive protocols with new ones that allow good urbanism to flourish, as if on well-constructed trellises. The "SmartCode" is a form-based code that replaces the segregated "Euclidean" zoning of an earlier era with a series of parametric specifications designed to ensure coherent streetscapes and public realms. The code uses a "transect" system to organize contextual responses to the urban condition, from the most intense urban setting to the most pristine natural environment.

But for Alexander, again, this kind of code does not address the core prerequisite of generativity, and without such guidance for growth the result is still likely to be well-aligned, lifeless junk. It prescribes a series of static parameters within which generative events may occur, but it does not in any way facilitate or guide their generation. Moreover, even to specify such parameters is to constrain the emergence of organic wholes, which require an environment in which adaptation of form can occur as needed.

Almost in response to the New Urbanists, it would seem, Alexander has proposed an alternate kind of code, based explicitly upon rule-based, generative processes of the kind outlined in 'A New Theory of Urban Design'. Alexander's generative code addresses not physical parameters of the built environment, but steps that the participants should take together in laying out and detailing a given structure. Alexander likens it to a recipe, or a medical procedure, in which the steps always follow a logically similar pattern, but the actual actions continuously adapt to the context – the taste and texture of the food in the case of a recipe, or the condition of the patient's tissues in a medical procedure. But in this case, the "recipe" or the "procedure" guides the unfolding of environmental form.

In its fullest form, this kind of generative code can be thought of as a design–build system, addressing all of the conditions of building – financing, ownership, management, sourcing, and, crucially, changes to the design along the way. For Alexander, the issue of cost control is a manageable process, and indeed, is done regularly within existing design–build approaches. He points out that much of the direction of technology is today aimed favourably for such an approach – one-off manufacturing, customisation, niche marketing, and so on. He is convinced of the possibility and even the inevitability of this transformation of technology, in a more adaptive, and ultimately, a more organic direction.

Duany's discussion of the "problem of large numbers" would find a sympathetic audience with the architect and theorist Rem Koolhaas. For Koolhaas – perhaps representing many other contemporary "neo-modernist" architects – the modern city is simply too complex to yield to a reform agenda like that of the New Urbanists. In the face of sheer quantity, architecture is powerless to change the direction of the urban wave, and therefore is wiser to seek merely to surf that wave with skill.

Koolhaas challenges Duany's faith in planning, and suggests that urbanism is now the art of accommodating generativity, rather than the futile attempt to design it: If there is to be a "new urbanism" it will not be based on the twin fantasies of order and omnipotence; it will be the staging of uncertainty; it will no longer be concerned with the arrangement of more or less permanent objects but with the irrigation of territories with potential; it will no longer aim for stable configurations but for the creation of enabling fields that accommodate processes that refuse to be crystallised into definitive form ... (Koolhaas 1995)

Or perhaps we need to look more deeply for a new paradigm within the insights of modern science and philosophy. This is precisely what Alexander has said he is seeking. In the planning disciplines, generativity has continued to develop in the work of other investigators. In particular, the trend toward engagement of residents evident in the third generation of the design methods movement has continued and accelerated.

For all their disagreements, the cross-fertilisations between Alexander's process advocates and the New Urbanists continue, with constructive results. The topic of generativity continues to loom large.

Duany's SmartCode – now adopted by dozens of municipalities and under consideration as the national planning code of Scotland, among others – has begun to take on some stepwise layout guides very similar to Alexander's. Duany argues that his code also incorporates many other aspects of generativity. For his part, Alexander has continued to develop his proposal for a "generative code," and to address the "massive process difficulties" that are posed by conventional building protocols, using many of the New Urbanists' insights.

Mehaffy's paper confirms the belief that the New Urbanists and the Neo-Modernists use the same thinking but with different slogans on their T-shirts, even though Koolhaas professes differently. No matter how hard we try to reconcile the differences between Alexander and the collective force of the two movements, we recognise that two fundamentally different thought processes are at work. One is from Venus and the other from Mars. The former has its roots in bottom -up individual response and the latter in top-down physical determinism. The former resonates with the self-builders, the latter with the established building industry. Most civilisations use standardised approaches: they call it vernacular. Most civilisations recognise individual expression, but within defined constraints. Both Alexander and Duany recognise the need for condition-making. They just disagree on how far you need to go.

In fact, we need both thinking and both approaches. We need bottom-up in combination with a different form of top-down. The real issue is at what scale and how do we achieve balance. Like most balanced systems we need to able to see them from different perspectives. They must be scaleable both up and down. Alexander should not become a New Urbanist but the New Urbanists must retreat from their entrenched positions to allow for a true vernacular to flourish and real unpredictability to occur. They can always advance, but from a stronger position. In our life, Venus needs Mars and Mars need Venus. The solution lies in the mutual recognition of both systems. At the moment the macho, autocratic and monopolistic dominance of Mars is suffocating the softer side of our Venus. Alexander is still our industry's lone suffragette.

SO WHERE ARE WE NOW?

Open source collaboration is a form of collective action that occurs when large numbers of people work independently on a single project, often modular in its nature using social software and computer-supported collaboration tools such as wiki technologies. A key aspect which distinguishes mass collaboration from other forms of large-scale collaboration, is that the collaborative process is mediated by the content being created - as opposed to direct social interaction. Organisations such as the Ashoka Foundation and the Natural Step see this as the only way forward to globalise knowledge and share experience.

A growing group of collaborators has assembled around this thinking agenda, and begun to pursue 'open-source' collaborations with biologists, ecologists, sociologists, behavioural and computer scientists and others. Such open source methods have yielded remarkable results for the computer software developers who exported Alexander's ideas into that realm with remarkable effect. Though progress has been slow the opportunity remains to develop further generative processes as a means to deliver more robust and more efficacious results – that is, more sustainable results – within the field of urban design.

As always, building emergent systems doesn't guarantee that they will turn out to be better than the old solutions. To succeed you need to get the conditions right.

We are searching for some kind of harmony between two intangibles: a form which we have not yet designed and a context which we cannot properly describe.

— Christopher Alexander

FIX

Smart Urbanism is an emerging proposition or equation: it is what our cities, towns and their districts, neighbourhoods and quarters need to respond to growth and change in an undefined future. Quite simply, it applies the 'theorem' with the 'thinking' using the 'tools' to fix the 'broken'.

Smart Urbanism is underpinned by five initiatives that we have used to develop and trial new processes and tools – Public Protocol, Urban ISM, The New Norm, The Popular Home and Neighbourhood Coefficient – all distinct but mutually supporting; each addressed to different audiences but still overlapping; and, each promoting a different code of behaviour but with the same outcome – making MASSIVE SMALL change.

THE CHALLENGE

The shifting paradigms point to the need for more complex thinking to solve the problems of exponential growth and change in cities, problems that cannot be solved with the urban design techniques we are using today. A new understanding therefore needs to be developed about the nature, scale and dynamics of spatial structure in relation to its context. Given the new imperatives, we need to consider how this can evolve from a bottom-up approach in order to meet this challenge.

This means looking to a different type of 'top-down' based on a more open, collaborative, systems-thinking approach – operating within a 'new essential order' that will create the medium for urban life, and therefore urban society, to emerge and flourish.

Open collaborative systems recognise that uncertainty and change make traditional top-down, command-and-control far less effective. Instead, the aim must be to adapt continuously to the environment. Open systems are therefore organic rather than mechanistic, and require a completely different mindset to run them. In these conditions, strategy and feedback are more important than detailed planning.

Openness simplifies complexity

—John Maeda, The Laws of Simplicity

Order is repetition of units.
Chaos is multiplicity without rhythm.

— M.C. Escher

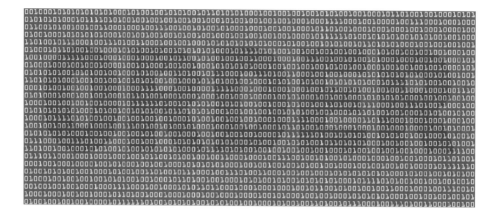

Regent's Quarter next to London's Kings Cross Station: diversity within a complex multi-use urban grain.

ENABLING MECHANISMS

What is now demanded, in addition to this 'new essential order', is the introduction of new processes that facilitate complexity into the design and management of our towns and cities. In the words of the urbanist, Romaldo Giurgola: "The problem of designing a city is different in nature to that of designing a building. To the sequence of box buildings we must oppose the plastic complexities of an architectural organism capable of generating urban fabric, or more simply, providing an alternative to monotony ...... In the past, patrons or civic leaders encouraged the rapid construction of only essential parts of the city: squares, harbours, acropolises and the like were created as pivots to the subsequent distribution (and infill) of operative and residential areas. These last grew voluntarily confused, thus retaining the secret of their private life. As a consequence they were highly habitable".

The 'new essential order' and the 'generators of urban fabric' are both enabling mechanisms that give structure to the city, providing the necessary framework of public action that will generate private reaction. These gestures in the public domain need to be fundamental and, coupled with a clear public direction, recognise that a framework of well-considered constraints provides the medium for creative response. This process cannot be completely rationalised or determined by analysis: its intention is, by means of synthesis, to create an environment that will always contain aspects of accident and disorder within its framework. It is not necessary to determine where to locate the pub, or how much retail space is required to sustain the local community. A successful urban fabric needs no functional programme. In fact, diversity within a complex multi-use urban grain becomes the ideal substitute for formal land-use planning. Alternative responses are then merely influenced by proximity of location or variety of place.

We need a new way of defining and regulating new development; something that focuses on the extra-small as the essential building block for our cities and towns. It is the cumulative effect of many 'extra-smalls' that will deliver the qualities we want from a place – the million dabs on the canvas, the fine-grain. This does not mean that everything needs to be small, but larger things should start from a combination of the small, always enabling the process of combination to be reversed.

Any new and essential order must recognise the importance of the ENABLING MECHANISMS for emergence and therefore complexity – the enabling spatial structure and networks, the generators and agents, the building blocks, dynamics and regularities, and the simple rules to guide change.

The real challenge lies in developing the tools to facilitate bottom-up processes in the planning, design and delivery of cities, towns and their districts, neighbourhoods and quarters. In learning from emergent systems and applying these to the qualities of successful urbanism we have come up with the concept of Smart Urbanism – a new paradigm that is constantly evolving as we continue to work on it.

A NEW OPERATING SYSTEM

Smart Urbanism is an operating system for delivering massive small change and, by definition, allowing the necessary complexity in the design of our towns and cities. It could be termed emergent urbanism or open source urbanism (or even sustainable, collaborative or generative urbanism) and certainly has the qualities of all. It comes from two agendas: firstly, the needs of the 'Resilient City' that looks to wider social, economic and environmental issues that good urban design can address and, secondly, the 'Talented City' where the need to foster innovation, facilitate enterprise and build social capital demand a more responsive urban fabric that is both resilient, accommodating of change and that we can programme over time. As such, it looks to put in place a new top-down discipline that is more 'open' to bottom-up responses from a range of actors. It also looks to limit choice but still allow infinite possibilities. It is therefore, by its very nature, freedom within constraints.

Smart Urbanism has its roots in the belief that uniqueness of place is reflected against the backdrop of a clearly defined urban order. This order, in turn, provides the necessary framework for urban variety and provides the palette for the "city of a thousand designers". This order is valid as an objective precisely because it becomes a mosaic for problem solving. While the underlying strategy is to extend and elaborate the structure and intensity of the city, there is recognition of its implicit unpredictability.

Smart Urbanism advances a form of urban ecology. It has seven drivers to foster emergence. All are overlapping and self-reinforcing. All are essential:

- COMPLEXITY: Places that offer the cumulative and collective benefits and consequences of many rich, varied and interrelated actions.

- COMPACTNESS: Places that capitalise on the immediate and collateral benefits of closeness, contiguity and concentration.

- CONNECTEDNESS: Places that offer a choice of movement modes, both to and through, as a consequence of coherent networks.

- COLLECTIVENESS: Places that foster civicness, sense of community, cohesiveness and build social capital through open systems.

- CO-EFFICIENCY: Places that factor in shared, supportive and symbiotic systems in building environmental capital in all aspects of daily life.

- CO-PRODUCTIVITY: Places that are open to emergence and change by facilitating a wide range of individual and collective actions.

- COOLNESS: Places that are comfortable, creative, and confident that have a strong sense of identity, ethics, values and cultural capital arising from their true authenticity.

The first six drivers are something we can foster. 'Coolness' is the consequence of the first six and you cannot design for it. It emerges.

CREATING THE RIGHT CONDITIONS

To the drivers of emergence we must add the most vital ingredient: the five CONDITIONS for emergence:

- RULES: [an agreed set of conditions, standards or actions],

- NETWORKS: [an interconnected, intricate or complex structure or lattice],

- FIELDS: [sets of elements or bit locations laid out in an orderly manner],

- DEFAULTS: [choices or settings that apply without active intervention],

- CATALYSTS: [agents that stimulate reaction, development or change].

Condition-making is what you do when you look to define the medium for urban life, culture, economy and environment to flourish. In doing so, you recognise that although you cannot plan endstates, you can put in place the preconditions for the endstate to be set in motion, monitored (with active feedback) and realised over time.

These conditions are our enabling mechanisms and, amplified by our five supporting initiatives, provide us with a clear set of interrelating and self-reinforcing processes and tools. These conditions are not necessarily sequential but can be used as a feedback loop. They are also not mutually exclusive. All are essential:

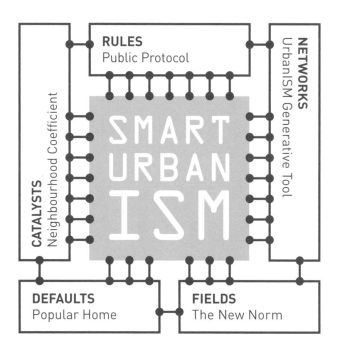

RULES [noun]: *an agreed set of conditions, standards or required actions*

CONDITION 1:
ESTABLISH SIMPLE RULES

Scientists have discovered that complex behaviour can result from a few simple rules. The most creative growth and change processes have a few simple rules, which reflect shared values and guide behaviour – the fewer the rules, the higher the creativity. People are also able to keep a small number of rules in mind, which helps them act on behalf of the city as its agents.

Complexity science is about finding simple rules that can generate complexity in the planning, design and delivery of our towns and cities. Scientists can decode simple rules from emergent systems that, even with modest means many will generate complexity and simultaneously solve a vast diversity of unique problems.

Without understanding how these rules create complexity, they simply repeat them after each successful building. This is exactly the field of work that urbanists should understand today, and from there we could allow maximum diversity in our cities without breaking symmetry and harmony.

> *The rules may be so simple that they may be easily codified into building regulation even by the dullest bureaucrats. Then again the behaviour may be so complex (that is to say there is emergence) that post-rationalised codification is even impossible, and the processes by which cities are governed may have to be completely reconsidered.*

—Stephen Wolfram

RULES AS TOOLS

Rules are everywhere – they are infrastructural. They hang like a fog over our built and non-built environments. They remain in force in locations that no street will ever reach. The dominate the air, just as they do the ground and that which lies beneath. As an abstract and immaterial urban infrastructure, they constitute a connection between built structures, land and its use.

Rules are universal and discrete guiding instruments, and they create an almost poetic, standardised irrationality.

—Alex Lehnerer

Rules are tools that can be used to guide us in structuring complex choices and achieving universal solutions. They give us our freedom within constraints. No society can manage without them. But, there are two types of rules that concern us:

1   rules as 'method' tools; and

2   rules as 'thinking' tools.

It is the second type that concerns us more in defining Smart Urbanism.

1. RULES AS METHOD TOOLS

We can hardly avoid acknowledging the significant role played by rules in shaping our cities, towns and their districts, neighbourhoods and quarters. In fact, the discipline of urban design – that is to say, the linking together of shared visions through the mediation of a variety of public and private sector interests – consists more of the conscious positing of rules than the drawing up of plans. Design codes are an example of this.

These types of tools are methodological tools are really well described in Alex Lehnerer's book. 'Grand Urban Rules' (2008). He says that in integrated, operational tools in planning and design, rules possess special qualities. Their implementation enables the precise formulation of degrees of freedom for specified areas and for the protagonists of the planning process. These freedoms are decisive for the generation of ephemeral qualities such as urban diversity, difference and vitality. Consciously deployed freedoms, moreover, endow planning with a certain sustainability and permanence in confronting an unpredictable future.

These types of rules are useful in structuring the design process and give us the means to evaluate it. They give us the design principles that can be applied to developing alternatives. They give us regularity and reliability. Some refer to norms or standards, others to procedures. Some are required minimums or maximums, others are preferred optimums. They can range from rigorous determinism to flexible interpretation. Quite often it is not the rules themselves that determine but the 'rules to break the rules' that are of more importance.

2. RULES AS THINKING TOOLS

These types of rules are valid at the higher level and shape our thinking before it becomes operational. They are more performance-based and enabling in nature. They are the rules that release the freedoms for multiple actions. They are also an essential part of the feedback loop – constantly learning, evolving and reinterpreting. From our understanding and thinking around emergent systems in life, business, information technology and choice architecture we can extract certain lessons. These are used to derive the simple rules that can be applied to achieving a better urbanism.

All these rules are mutually self-reinforcing. All are valid. So, if you don't accept the default settings (spoken about later in this chapter), follow the rules on the next page.

Simple, clear purpose and principles give rise to complex and intelligent behaviour. Complex rules and regulations give rise to simple and stupid behaviour.

—Dee Hock

1. LIMITING CHOICE < INFINITE POSSIBILITIES

This rule stresses the need for narrowing down choices as a precondition to emergent behaviour. Using effective mechanisms to narrow choices is something evolved societies have always done. Structuring complex choices gives infinite possibilities. Without a limiting of choice, decisions are not made and self-organisation stalls. Defaults and incentives are a way of influencing choice.

2. INCENTIVISING THE FINE GRAIN

To foster emergence we need mechanisms (the building blocks, generators and agents) and perpetual novelty. In urbanism these lie in the urban grain of a settlement. This rule implies that you need to subdivide and retain the smallest building blocks of cities. The grain needs protection and incentivising. Consolidation of the grain is seen as a brake.

3. WE WILL, IF YOU WILL

This rule recognises that citizens' moral and/or political obligations are dependent upon a contract or agreement among them to form the society in which they live. In a bottom-up world, new roles and relationships are formed and we need new social contracts between local government and community. The words 'We will, if you will' establish the simple rules for emergence to be derived.

4. SMALL CHANGE = BIG DIFFERENCE

This rule encapsulates the concept of sensitive dependence on initial conditions – a beating butterfly wing can create the potential for a tornado. Small changes upstream in a complex system can have large effects elsewhere. Distributed networks have shown that a small number of rules or laws can generate incredibly complex systems. Small changes or 'nudges' can lead to big differences.

5. HARDWARE + SOFTWARE + INTERFACES

This rule recognises that multiple interactions require the hardware of physical form, the software of programmes and an easily understandable operating system. Many consider urbanism something purely physical and formal, but we should definitely take a look at the soft side of the city and recognise those non-physical structures as shapers of their districts, neighbourhoods and quarters.

6. UPSCALE/DOWNSCALE

This rule sees scalability is a desirable property of a system, a network, or a process, which indicates its ability to either handle growing complexity in a graceful manner or to be enlarged or reduced without changing the fundamental principles and values of the system. This rule is essential to offering choice over time – a prerequisite of incremental and organic growth and change.

7. LONG LIFE/LOOSE FIT

This rule applies to the robustness of a place and the ability of a system to adapt itself efficiently and to fast changing circumstances. An adaptive system is therefore an open system that is able to fit its behaviour according to changes in its environment or in parts of the system itself. Long life, loose-fit' displaces 'form follows function' as a construct. Universal space becomes more important as a measure.

8. INDEPENDENCE + INTERCHANGEABILITY

This rule states that many multiple actions require simple processes that accommodate maximum flexibility for changing behaviours. It stresses the importance of ensuring non-sequential, independent timelines for any individual or collective action. Interchangeability needs modular systems with standardised units or dimensions for flexibility and variety in use is a key to facilitating massive small change.

9. BOTTOM-UP NEEDS TOP-DOWN

This rule states that you can have top-down without bottom-up: but bottom-up needs top-down, albeit with a different mindset. Collaborative systems recognise that traditional top-down, command-and-control do not work in this context and managing complexity must be open and hierarchical if it is to be effective. The new top-down gives the 'light touch' essential order necessary to avoid confusion.

10. LEADERSHIP MUST BE ENABLING

This rule states that open systems are therefore organic rather than mechanistic, and require a completely different mindset to run them. The role of traditional civic leadership grows less effective in bottom-up systems – less concerned with establishing a direction for the city, and more involved with enabling activity that generates the best ideas. Strategy and feedback are more important than detailed planning.

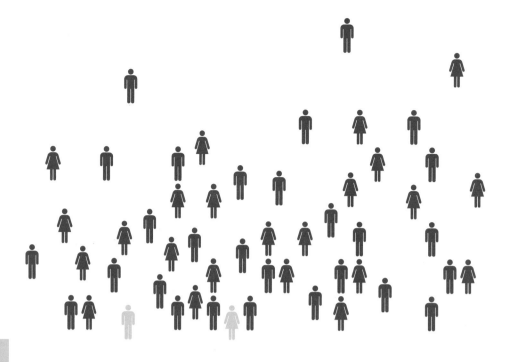

Why the big secret? People are smart; they can handle it.

"A person is smart. People are dumb, panicky and dangerous animals, and you know it."

—Will Smith and Tommy Lee Jones, Men in Black

FIX

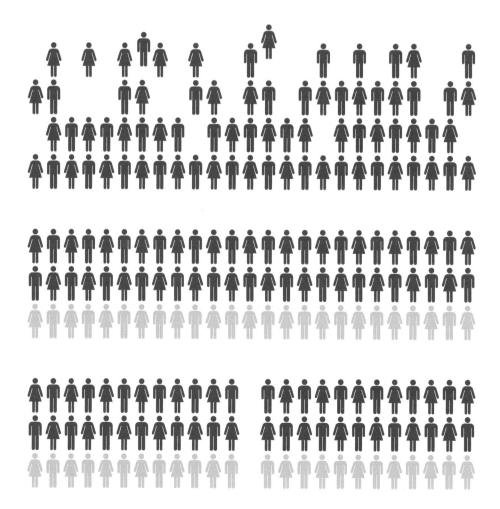

PUBLIC PROTOCOL

With the right skills, local communities can be smart as well. They should be able to create effective systems that will help govern and shape their own development in new kinds of ways: the "eyes on the street" that Jane Jacobs celebrated in her classic works on urbanism, now amplified by the communication capabilities and web-based tools of the networked age. Just as the ants find their way to new food sources and switch tasks with impressive flexibility, our community tools should help us locate and improve troubled schools, up-and-coming playgrounds, areas lacking crucial services, areas with an abundance of services, blocks that feel safe at night and blocks that don't – all the subtle patterns of community life now made public in a new form.

'Public Protocol' is a working method for enabling our communities to deliver positive growth and change. It has been developed over the years by Urban Initiatives as its 'way' and is a tried and tested (and constantly evolving) mechanism for entering into new social contracts with the communities affected by regeneration and renewal. It is pure localism at work, enabling neighbourhood teams to be truly involved in the planning, design and delivery processes by giving them the tools to take action and have genuine sway in their neighbourhoods. It can be difficult to achieve community collaboration but from our understanding of self-organising systems, we acknowledge four basic principles of behaviour that are needed to promote open collaboration:

- The first principle is 'self-organisation'. Through the basic mechanisms of decentralised control, distributed problem-solving and multiple interactions, a community without being told can transform simple rules of thumb into meaningful patterns of collective behaviour.

- The second principle is 'diversification of knowledge' – which is basically achieved through a broad sampling of options, followed by a friendly competition of ideas. Then using an effective mechanism to narrow down the choices, communities can achieve 'wisdom of crowds'. By adopting this principle, they can build trust and make better decisions.

- The third principle is 'indirect collaboration'. If individuals in a community are prompted to make small changes to a shared structure or idea that inspires others to improve it even further, the structure or idea becomes an active player in the creative process.

- The fourth principle is 'dissemination'. The basic mechanisms of coordination and communication can unleash powerful waves of energy or awareness that race across a community to evoke positive change.

Collaboration does not happen with seeding it. Language is used to both inform and baffle... professionals often use their language as their 'black box'... but language can also empower! The best way to equip a local neighbourhood team with the right skills is through capacity building – giving it the language that is used in the professional world (not dumbing down the process), so that it can shape ideas and proposals from the very outset.

THE NEIGHBOURHOOD GAME

There is no substitute to leading from the front, armed with understanding and tactical acumen. Such is the way of successful cities, towns and their districts, neighbourhoods and quarters. We have developed an interactive 'game' as our effective mechanism to narrow down the choices in neighbourhood transformation and simulate potential outcomes. It helps to explore the relationship between sustainability, the density of development and its investment value, in this way informing decision-making. The Neighbourhood Game can be adapted to different places and issues and can be played with a range of people, from residents to council officers or even elected members.

The game board is based on an aerial photograph of the place and playing tiles are used to represent different types of development, such as homes, community facilities, parks, shops and offices. These playing tiles can be placed on the board to explore where new development could take place, the appropriate balance of uses and the implications in terms of delivery and funding.

There are now a number of versions of the game – we know that it works. It's a great way to get people talking about specific issues that are important to them and introduce a friendly competition of ideas. It avoids the usual pitfalls of community involvement by encouraging those involved to think realistically about how their needs and desires will be delivered on the ground. Through this process it structures and builds shared ideas that can be easily disseminated to a wider audience.

We can use the Neighbourhood Game to sample options, thus enabling the team to understand the design and development process and how informed trade-offs can be made to ensure that the project is built. This is the right way of doing community collaboration and real benefits will flow from using these approaches and techniques. Not only will we be able to meet the goals of localism, but more importantly the Public Protocol can help to achieve successful regeneration in which communities are given the power to shape their own futures.

The Neighbourhood Game at work in the Aylesbury Estate, South London (2008)

WHAT ARE THE NEW BEHAVIOURS?

Simple rules demand a fundamental shift in behaviour in all aspects of planning design and delivery. For many this is serious paradigm shift!

A. FOR PLANNING

The biggest implication for planning lies in the recognition that the 'predict-and-provide' method of determining growth and change will not work anymore. It means developing a new understanding of the simple rules outlined previously and applying these to everyday problems.

For those set in their ways this is difficult. For those who want to do what they set out to do as planners, and make the world a much better place, this is nirvana – they are empowered to act. The role of the planner becomes 'enabling' not 'permitting'. Planning stops being a game where applicants, as they more than often say, play against a team with eleven goalkeepers – development control becomes development facilitation. Continuous feedback is imperative so information is king.

For planning this means a different relationship with the community. Here planners are fellow collaborators and this means they must arm the civic leaders and wider community with a better understanding of the sense of the possible. Change must be framed in the context of community building (not as development) with the benefits of change being transparently linked to action.

B. FOR DESIGN

Efforts are directed to designing interchangeable, modular systems of development. Design is not a static solution – it evolves and self-perfects. Good design percolates down to many. Potential is still released for the special but it is defined within the construct of a 'vernacular'. Districts, neighbourhoods and quarters are assembled and cities flourish. Finally design makes a real difference.

C. FOR DELIVERY

There is now a greater focus on the 'Local'. For procurement it means managing multiple actions by many players. More authority and responsibility is given to those empowered to facilitate delivery and make the necessary nudges. The latent potential of the collective is mobilised. Systems are more transparent and micro-concerns become important. Longer term stewardship is the key.

NETWORK [noun]: *Any interconnecting structure or lattice that is intricately formed or complex*

CONDITION 2:
CREATE INTELLIGENT NETWORKS

This condition gives rise to the coarse web – the sticky lattice of urban life – that is the essential building block of cities and their districts, neighbourhoods and quarters and functions as the primary generator of urban form. It gives us complexity, connectedness and sows the seeds for compactness.

Success of any incremental transformation will depend on the creation of a significant and essential open but hierarchical order – an urban network imbued with choice at a variety of levels. Such an order could be established through the application of a simple urban structure that possesses certain concrete qualities. It may also be defined in terms of how things are structured in relation to one another (though this may be more difficult to define).

Although we may move to more local and independent systems, infrastructure networks do impose a regulating order that is difficult to overcome and exert a strong influence on the shape of our urban fabric. Notwithstanding this, we have to create the conditions for urban life, culture and economy to flourish and that means defining the medium within which this can occur.

We can't get away without defining any order. Even relational systems need some structure and rules. We should not be scared of imposing an order. Traditional societies have done this well: defining freedom within constraints – the limiting of choice which gives rise to infinite possibilities.

THE EVOLUTION OF THE NETWORK

The NETWORK has three stages of evolution from its initial definition of its structure, through its evolution to the mobilisation as an effective and functioning system.

STAGE 1: DEFINE THE BACKBONE

This gives the essential diagram of the place: the ten strokes of a pen on a plan – defining major routes, public transport infrastructure, the institutions for civic life, and zones of development and urban edges. At a city scale, this is the first trigger for an emergent urbanism. Some uses aggregate to accessibility, others to similar uses and yet others to the need for some form of prominence. At a neighbourhood scale it is the high street, the market, the civic spaces.

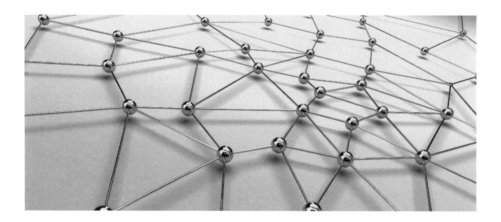

FIX

STAGE 2: EVOLVE THE NETWORK

Once a backbone is in place the process of network formation can begin by creating an open grid of connected secondary streets and blocks laid out in a hierarchical order. This is the pattern of the city and its parts: the park, the super-block, the soft-centred block, the mews block and the street block – the building blocks of the district, quarter or neighbourhood. This stage is the lowest order of defining complexity; the highest receptor for emergence and the first point that local social and economic clusters form.

STAGE 3: MOBILISE THE STREET

At the local level, the street is the primary generator of the neighbourhood. The fundamental configuration of a street – a movement axis lined by buildings with their entrances facing each other – is not in the first instance derived from issues of style or tradition. It is the result of an emergent order derived from inherent qualities of geometry that maximise integration of movement patterns and thus maximises the potential for human interaction. This is why the street can be found across a range of cultures and throughout history. Every street needs a function that contributes to the accretion of urban fabric. Movement is like a channel of glue. It is not the flow down this channel that sticks things together, it is the stopping. That is why in the early formation of a neighbourhood we cannot waste any adhesiveness, never mind the energy and costs, on roads that have no function other than to bypass.

THE IMPORTANCE OF OPEN ADAPTIVE SYSTEMS

Whatever form the network of the city takes – regular or distorted, orthogonal or radial, celebratory or modest – it must have the qualities of openness and hierarchy, both essential for fostering complexity and structuring complex choices. In planned urbanism we cannot recreate the organic nature of the village, but we can create the conditions that give rise to organic transformation. If we wish to design for diversity, however, we have much to gain from learning to recognise nuances in traditional planned cities and towns: its origins and initial intents, how differences in it have developed, how our building and environmental management policies may in turn affect it, and how we can better respect or enhance differences which already exist between one area and another. We can learn to see street layouts not merely as a sterile initial plan but as a collection of artefacts, which reveal the processes of urban building.

The geometry of the open hierarchical grid has long been advocated as providing the necessary framework for urban variety. Our most successful models for planned growth are those where the positive qualities of the grid have been exploited in combination with squares, mews and boulevards. In this sense we are not talking about the American supergrid, such as seen in cities like Philadelphia. This type of grid demonstrates openness but not hierarchy.

Most successful planned cities are collisions of mini-grids or combinations of formal grid patterns. We are talking of examples we can see around us every day in great cities and their districts, neighbourhoods and quarters: the regular hierarchical Georgian grids of Mayfair or Fitzrovia in London; the highly-evolved complex grids of Edinburgh New Town and Savannah in Georgia. All of these demonstrate the potential to accommodate urban variety at a number of scales and have served us well, adapting to change over the years and perpetually demonstrating regularity and novelty. They can take the extraordinary and the normal. They are both the foreground and the background of an essential order.

It is remarkable that many spontaneous urban settlements, given the total freedom to arrange themselves how and where they want, organise themselves into open hierarchical systems that endure well into their formalisation as districts, neighbourhoods and quarters of the city or town. Most are complex social, economic and movement networks. Most are grids.

The present traffic planning system is dominated by the pseudo-scientific constructs of the current closed 'hierarchy of roads' policy, such that the proposals for open hierarchical grids draws opposition from old school die-hards. Open grids fly full in the face of the established tree-like diagrams of our traffic engineers. The tree is not a complex network and therefore does not easily offer different interpretations. For us to move on, this thinking needs to change, and this is not just a matter of defining hierarchies through reference to factors other than just traffic. It will require us to recognise that the nature or character of any given street can vary significantly along its length and is likely change over time.

THE GRID AS THE GENERATOR OF FORM

In 'A City is not a Tree', Christopher Alexander shows that successful social and economic networks form complex lattice patterns, but that observers limited their interpretations to a simple mathematical tree of segregated parts and sub-parts, eliminating many connections in the process. The same can be said for movement systems. In attempting to plan for urban structure, a single human mind falls back on tree diagrams to maintain their conceptual control of the plan, thus computing well below the level of spontaneous urban complexity.

To dispel many of the myths propagated by the Garden City movement, Paul Groth refers to the following articles of 'pro-grid creed of faith':

- **Article 1**: The grid can be a symbol of positive and human values. The grid historically has been a common symbol not for greed but for rational urban life symbolising the achievement of relative egalitarianism.

- **Article 2**: Viable human settlements with a proper sense of community can thrive on a grid plan as well as any other form and, for the newcomer, the comprehensibility of the grid can be a source of security.

- **Article 3**: Grids do not necessarily create mechanical monotony in urban design and may, in fact, be the best possible provision for organic growth in a city's future. Further, the grid has adapted itself well to long periods of growth and change.

- **Article 4**: The grid allows but does not cause high density. Grids are indeed the most efficient forms of compact settlement, but the decision to build compactly should be seen as policy not as a result of street form.

To this we can now add:

- **Article 5**: The grid, when having the qualities of an open hierarchical network, provides the essential order for emergence. Hierarchical redesign of grids is therefore a diversifying process.

It is the definition of a grid that will largely define the city shape. The specific procedure of each designer finds different ways of applying such grids basing their decisions on different criteria. Decisions on the grid dimensions come from experience and tacit knowledge. What this means is that certain patterns relate the grid dimensions with the characterisations of the types of blocks and neighbourhood, producing different links for future phases of the design. At this point, the chosen patterns generate designs for the transportation and street networks and movement systems.

It is the processes of change – design, initial settlement, social specialisation, accretion, evolution of infrastructure systems and traffic management – that give the grids their subtle but real variety. Although only one of many formal and social contexts in which urban architecture can take place, the open hierarchical grid is nonetheless the most robust and adaptable form of physical structure.

SMART NETWORKS

'Smart' has become the umbrella term for making the best possible use of new technologies and new ideas to make life better in urban areas. Whether it is London's Oyster card, sustainable housing, low-carbon schemes or the targeted delivery of public services online in order to save energy and time, innovation can create intelligent networks for all.

A smart grid is a form of intelligent network utilising digital technology and is being promoted as a way of addressing complex energy dependence and resilience issues. It thrives on a lattice formation. Its principles can be applied to local energy networks, water management and information technology. Recognising that traffic models cannot deal with the complexity of urban traffic monitoring and management systems, engineers are now exploring the potential for grids to take on the principle of self-learning, with traffic controls adjusting to peak flow conditions in intelligent ways.

Constructing the smart and sustainable city of the future – and making existing ones smarter – raises new challenges for planning, design and delivery processes. Developers are now required not to simply think in isolation but to make their buildings synchronise in a holistic fashion with other components of the urban toolbox – transport and utilities providers as well as the digital world – while also making them energy efficient and sustainable at the same time.

A smart city is an open city. It runs on data, so public bodies need to demonstrate a presumption of openness, making data freely available online in an accessible format. Data connectivity needs to be seen as a right, not a privilege and as ubiquitous as water from the tap. As Drew Hemment, director of Future Everything says:

> *Do not turn to futurologists with glib visions... The smart city is about connectivity: connectivity of systems, devices, data, people, organisations. Connectivity between all kinds of things, on all kinds of levels. To those charged with creating the smart cities of the future is this: invest in connectivity (and bandwidth) and build up your social capital – trust, intelligence, opportunity. Community is king.*

Technology cannot replace common sense as most of the challenges are social, not technical. You need a critical mass of people creating ideas and solutions. Community is the long game because active and engaged communities build sustainability into the system. Local authorities need to shift out of a top-down service delivery mindset to let the new smart ecosystem evolve, rich in complexity. It is going to be built by many people, working in different ways and on different levels.

Cities will be key drivers for this agenda, and there is a sweet spot between cities that are small enough for co-ordinated action and large enough to achieve a critical mass. But it is around LOCALITIES [districts, neighbourhoods and quarters], with their efficiencies of scale and their relative fleetness of foot, that the lasting effects of change will be realised and happen quickly.

According to Wikipedia, Smart cities exist along six main axes or dimensions: a smart economy; smart mobility; a smart environment; smart people; smart living; and, finally, smart governance. These six axes connect with traditional regional and neoclassical theories of urban growth and development. In particular, the axes are based - respectively - on theories of regional competitiveness, transport and ICT economics, natural resources, human and social capital, quality of life, and participation of citizens in the governance of cities. A city can be defined as 'smart' when investments in human and social capital and traditional and modern communication infrastructure fuel sustainable economic development and a high quality of life, with a wise management of natural resources, through participatory governance.

FIX

In most cases we will not be building brand new cities, but building on top of old infrastructure, retrofitting the future, but the current euphoria, however, centres around a more radical vision. Rather than retrofitting old cities, the proposition is to build entire smart or 'intelligent' cities from scratch in a matter of a few years. Masdar City in Abu Dhabi, which is under construction, is an example of this and is conceived as an urban model for the future: solar powered, car-free, zero-carbon. It is a laboratory: a piece of real life that functions as a window, allowing us to learn about a fully intelligent and green city. Building such a city is a daunting proposition, particularly one that puts all that technology truly at the service of the inhabitants – and not, as in many instances, the other way around.

According to Saskia Sassen in her article 'Talking Back to the Intelligent City' in the McKinsey Journal, the aspect of intelligent cities is exciting. The city becomes a living laboratory for smart urban technologies that can handle all the major systems a city requires: water, transport, security, garbage, green buildings, and clean energy. The act of installing, experimenting, testing, or discovering – all of this can generate innovations. It could lead to a new type of open-source network, where there would be a collective upgrading and problem-solving dimension involving citizens: a sort of open-source urbanism. Sassen sees the need to push this technology further, and in different directions. Urbanising these intelligent cities would help them live longer because they would only then be capable of being truly open systems, subject to ongoing changes and further innovations.

Masdar City, Abu Dhabi

WHAT DOES THE CITY OF THE FUTURE LOOK LIKE?

The smartest city of them all will be PlanIT Valley, planned near Porto in Portugal, by Living PlanIT, founded by Steve Lewis, formerly of Microsoft. What makes it different is that it is more about smart urbanism than smart systems. The concept is to build intelligent networks that combine diverse insertable and removable electronic services. In other words, interchangeability – maintaining hardware and software systems with reusable components as needs change. In this way, rather than allowing the technology to control the urban environment, the environment shapes the technology.

> *Cityness is one way of opening up the category and allowing for more variability in what constitutes urbanity. This generates a whole field for research and interpretation, and invites us to reposition our notions of what cities should look like and to explore a far broader range of building technologies and urban spaces.*
>
> —Saskia Sassen

The key question is do intelligent networks demand a new urban form or configuration for the city or does conventional urbanity still prevail. It is interesting to note that Masdar City, despite having a rabbit warren of underground infrastructure, still looks like a hierarchical open grid – a more intensive Chandigarh. Songho in Seoul, another smart city, is traditional downtown. It would appear that at city scale, technology does not shape; it is servant to the plan. At neighbourhood scale it is slightly different. Energy networks do impose a rigour on the plan but these can be readily accommodated within the open hierarchical system.

Sustainable, innovative and fully-wired, the new urban metropolis will revolutionise the way we organise ourselves – individually and by community, they say. The result will be truly 'smart' cities that use technology to make our lives better. The continual fear is always that a technology driven-approach will result in Future Shock, Blade Runner, Buckminster Fuller (and all that). Also, what about civic governance and how do we prevent a new form of economic feudalism?

But, whenever we have had a leap in technology, cities have urbanised further. People may choose to work differently but just look at the effect of free wi-fi on the development of our cultural quarters and coffee houses: hardly a collapse of urbanity? Talent still wants to socialise.

Technology gives us the ability to be flexible, to give us infinite possibilities to forward fund projects against later revenues. We need to make good decisions that get us the public good outcomes we are trying to achieve. What we need to do is see our city and neighbourhood plans as our 'motherboards'. These enable places to go through change but to still have a fundamental order – plug-and-play comes to mind. In this way we can wire up our cities to suit, add new processors and memory and boot up.

GENERATIVE URBANISM

We now know that urban design processes need to adopt flexible and adaptive procedures to respond to the evolving demands of the contemporary city. To support these dynamics, as well as monitor conditions, we need specific design methods and the tools to support them. Urban designers have some tools at their disposal however these are certainly lacking in usefulness and meaning in complex urban environments – for example, using a 400-metre walk band as a determinant. This tool is classic reductionism: the great unchallenged truth in urban design that fails to acknowledge the complexity of the city. What is missing is a process tool that offers design information as well as feedback, the essential ingredient for bottom-up approaches.

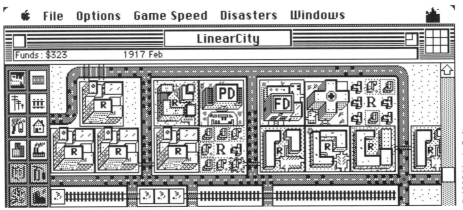

We know that if we can get the structure of a place right we can use different techniques to generate urban form and even give us clues to transforming neighbourhoods. This is not necessarily as end states but rather to anticipate outcomes such as how much land we need, the nature of infrastructure investment or provision of local services. The tools could test such variables as public transport accessibility to determine the nature and extent of services over time. They could be used to identify thresholds for energy networks or for carbon footprinting. They could also be used to identify thresholds for the provision of public services and model public good outcomes. They could even be used to simulate neighbourhood formation.

SimCity offers us some clues as to how we could do this but it is still not a generative model. It follows relatively simple rules, and projects these rules out over an infinite number of interacting agents. At present it is still difficult to model the whole city, given its sheer complexity, but given enough interactions, and given the right simple rules, the simulated neighbourhood can emerge.

We have been experimenting with a set of tools: Urban ISM (Integrated Spatial Model) and the Neighbourhood Game, which look to basic forms of simulation, using the principles of Smart Urbanism. Using simple rules we can assist the community in making complex decisions around trade-offs, having armed them with a number of 'rules' they can control. This is an iterative process and is not intended to gives us a final outcome but rather to chart a course of action that we can monitor feedback and adapt over time.

An early version of SimCity on Mac OS 6.0

FIX

Urban designers and local authorities could really benefit from further research into the most appropriate rules in this domain, thus moving it from the realms of gaming to real life applications. Generative urban design needs the development of a design system or process rather than a single design solution. The answer lies in an amalgamation of systems. Geographic Information Systems (GIS) are a very powerful system for accessing large-scale urban data; hence they play an important role in urban planning as an analytical tool: however they were conceived as interactive maps and so they lack capacities for designing. On the other hand, Computer-Aided Design (CAD) systems are very powerful drawing tools and fit for design practice.

In urban design, the linking of GIS to CAD tools becomes an important goal, as this will allow designing directly on the GIS data. This design process uses pre-existing GIS data as a starting point and the generation of designs will involve the application of the rules codified in patterns. Moreover, this toolkit will allow the designer to create designs that respect these patterns rather than simply repeating them.

GENERATIVE MODELS

Beirão and Duarte in their paper 'Structuring a Generative Model for Urban Design' (2007) see urban design as the result of applying a set of urban patterns and 'method' rules that can be applied at four different scales or development phases, separately or together.

A Rules based on a city scale, through an analysis of the existing settlement, establish the relevant clues for the definition of the plan's structural geometries.

B The urban grids or city tissue, lay down the remaining features of the street structure.

C The norms of the place determine the characteristics of the urban elements, such as the neighbourhood, blocks, lots and plots.

D The detailing of the urban space, which defines its material aspects, ambiences and other details.

A set of urban patterns defines a vision for a certain scale of the urban design problem. Each urban pattern may produce different 'method' rules, meaning each designer will define his own interpretation for that pattern based on his preferences.

In 'A Pattern Language' (Alexander et al, 1977), each pattern is an individual entity that identifies a recurrent problem in our environment, and points out the solution to that problem in such way that it can be used many times without having exactly the same outcome. Alexander proposes the idea that patterns can be modified and refined according to specific situations and environments: opening a wide field of concepts for exploring design. Furthermore, the idea provides the possibility of creating new patterns for new districts, neighbourhoods and quarters.

Alexander's patterns were criticised for their lack of precision or structure at a finer level, but this was at a time when we did not have the power of computers to assist us.

To allow a suitable structure for computing, Beirão and Duarte proposed a refined pattern structure to solve specific design problems and make design solutions more flexible and reusable. Their approach uses the same principles as any programming language. This upgrade to the 'pattern language' theory points a way of linking a mostly theoretical side of a really good pattern concept developed by Alexander, to a precise structure, suitable for computational purposes.

MANIPULATING COMPLEXITY
Bill Hillier and his colleague at University College London, Mike Batty, have developed a number of methodologies to analyse and manipulate complexity in our towns and cities. Their insights clearly draw from the rapid developments in complexity science in general. Investigators have been able to identify with mathematical precision the processes that give rise to complex structures from an apparently simple set of rules, with useful implications for game theory, economics, biology, physics, meteorology, and many other fields. In the fields of planning and urban design, the insights can be used to understand the relationship between complex urban form and relatively simple generative rules – like those followed by a group of actors in a building process. The significance of Hillier's and Batty's tools is that they have applied these insights to the urban toolkit available to practitioners, in effect to regenerate the urban complexity that previously existed or could potentially exist, with desirable results. Hillier's analytical technique, 'Space Syntax' in particular, has been put to the test a number of times with notable success.

To build up an effective generative tool for urban design purposes we need to refine this approach into one better adapted for design rather than analysis, or where analysis is part of the continuous feedback process. This is the 'golden egg' of urban design. We are not here yet but we are getting there.

URBAN ISM

Urban ISM is a tool for measuring and delivering the 'Networks' of Smart Urbanism at a range of settlement scales. It's a new geodesign application, bringing GIS and design processes together with the qualities of land use mix, accessibility and land value as part of an integrated process for spatial planning and urban design at multiple scales.

The system allows users to test development scenarios, giving real time data on the development performance. This reduces project time and risk and gives clients a more responsive approach to large-scale urban design and spatial planning projects. It can be used by all built environment professions, often working best as a collaborative project tool.

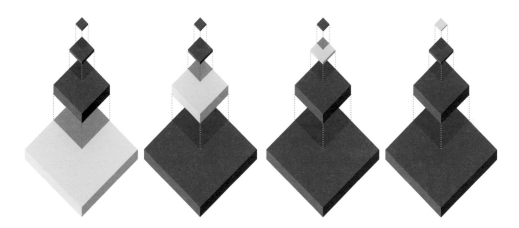

GAMING AS A GENERATIVE PROCESS

Through the 'neighbourhood game' interface, the system can be used as part of community or neighbourhood planning events and is therefore ideally suited to the new Localism agenda. For large-scale engagement, the tool can be used as a physical gaming board and screen projection. It operates across a range of urban scales from the whole town or city through to district and neighbourhood and has been designed to test the implications of large and medium scale urban changes. At a large scale, Urban ISM is able test the effects of urban extensions, mixed use development, public transport corridors, brownfield development and town centre redevelopment. At a medium scale the system can assess the implications of new social infrastructure such as schools or hospitals, as well as area wide transport strategies.

To simplify data entry, data is managed through a grid and tile system. The approach works across a number of scales and allows grids to be tailored to the study area. At whole town or city scale, we often adopt a 500m tile (25Ha). For projects focusing on urban extensions a 200m tile (4 Ha) is used. At neighbourhood level or for smaller settlements, smaller grain tiles of 100m (1Ha), 50m or 15m are best. For some of our transport and streets projects, a link (vector) based system is used.

Both pages: Urban Integrated Spatial Model (ISM) at work with its scales of intervention.

Urban ISM doesn't design masterplans – good designers do that. It's more about direction setting at an early stage, or at any stage if things don't seem to stack up. It helps set project tone and direction through a better understanding of land use mix, density, social infrastructure, accessibility, value and sustainability choices. It can be used over time to chart masterplan progress; co-ordinate infrastructure delivery; and provide continuous feedback to enable early decisions to be made. It can be used to test new development, reconsider planned but yet undelivered development or seek to optimise existing places through small scale and incremental change.

The following modules have been developed to test four of the key drivers of Smart Urbanism:

FIX

COMPLEXITY MODULE
Land use diversity
Measures the number of different land uses within a defined area

Social infrastructure
Determines the need and thus viability of services such as schools, health and local retail

Land use accessibility and catchment
A measure of pedestrian access based on permeability of the network and its catchment population

CONNECTEDNESS MODULE
Grid Permeability
Measures the ability to move through a grid tile in multiple directions based on actual highway network

Public Transport Accessibility
Measure of bus and rail frequency combined with walk access

Public Transport Viability
A measure of potential public transport demand and viability

Highway Access
A measure of traffic accessibility to the major road network

COMPACTNESS MODULE
Population density + compactness
Measures residential population per grid tile and neighbourhood compactness based on the proximity of the surrounding population

Urban Intensity
A measure of daytime population concentration

COEFFICIENT MODULE
Travel Emissions
A measure of transport CO_2 emissions associated with 'travel to work' based on development mode share and distance forecast

Energy Emissions
Measure of CO_2 emissions associated with residential/ commercial energy consumption and potential for sustainable community power generation

WHAT ARE THE NEW BEHAVIOURS?

All of the above mechanisms require a fundamental shift in behaviour in planning, design and delivery, some more radical than others. The most radical shift is that which deals with our old predictive models. The most important is how we deal with the complex issues of infrastructure in an emerging system. This is where research needs to be focused in the future.

A. FOR PLANNING

For connected networks this means a return to the urban structure plans that clearly set out the future growth and change web – identifying the links, joining the dots, preserving the corridors – just keeping the system open. Some of the worst mistakes that have been made in recent years have been in not keeping future options open. This will avoid the unconnected places of the recent past and ensure that we have the enabling framework for successful urbanism. The biggest shift will be towards more physical planning and design, not just words!

Using generative methods and tools with feedback loops will enable planners to continuously test scenarios and develop investment plans for future growth and change. Push and push-back become the norm. There will be long term visions but open systems will mean shorter term responsive actions.

B. FOR DESIGN

This means constantly recognising that any new addition to the city is not an end state. Others will need to connect in later. For designers it means a greater focus on grid structures – complex and simple – creating the conditions for emergence wherever possible. For traffic engineers it means throwing out your old models and thinking in complex ways. You cannot predict-and-provide, so recognise this. For urban designers it means getting smarter with generative methods. We are so close to getting these right. All we need are the simple rules.

C. FOR DELIVERY

The single biggest challenge lies in how new infrastructure networks are funded and how we deal with the heat and energy networks in the context of the carbon challenge. Increasingly, energy companies are willing to fund infrastructure in return for guaranteed revenue streams. This is like giving away free phones so you can link someone into a long term contact.

In Portugal, PlanIT are looking to build a whole city based on this business model. Like Hammarby in Sweden, why can't local authorities also take on this role? This could set the tone for a new way of plan-making and civic governance. Carefully considered, it could also be a complete and compelling new way of delivering smart urbanism at a massive scale.

FIELD [noun]: *A set of elements laid out in an orderly manner, a set of bit locations*

CONDITION 3:
DEFINE EMERGENT FIELDS

When Charles Mason and Jeremiah Dixon sailed to Philadelphia with their commission to survey America, they had the most powerful tool at their disposal: that of the 'boundary'. Their job was to create order and with it define the new fields for emergent behaviour.

It is the 'field' that gives rise to the fine grain – the DNA or cellular structure of the place – by breaking down the city and its districts, neighbourhoods and quarters into the building blocks for complexity and therefore emergence. We can see these fields as the Petri dish: the medium where we can grow life, economy and culture. By breaking down the city into its smallest elements we release the potential for multiple interactions and creations by many actors: making massive small change.

It is the process of breaking down the big into the small that gives us clues to how we deal with our large sites, either inner city or, more particularly, on the outskirts of many of our towns and cities. In doing this we can find solutions to monopolising practices that offer only single formula approaches and open up the market to a wider range of responses: More of lots progressively rather than lots of more excessively.

> *The building of cities is one of man's greatest achievements. The form of his city always has been and always will be a pitiless indicator of the state of his civilisation.*

—Edmund N. Bacon

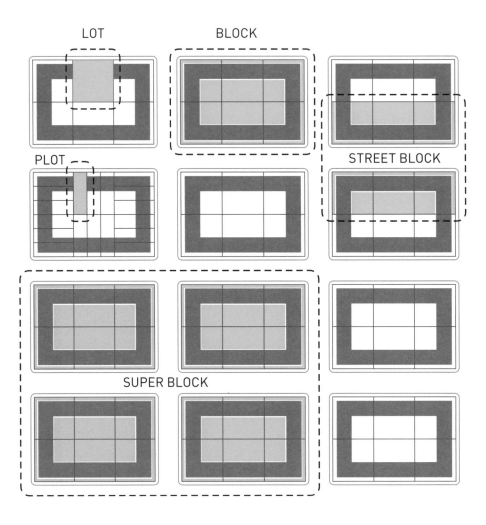

LOT · BLOCK · STREET BLOCK · PLOT · SUPER BLOCK

The key set of elements: PLOT<LOT>BLOCK

WHAT ARE THE SET OF ELEMENTS?

These are the plot, the lot and the block – something laid out in an orderly manner. These lie in the lost art of subdivision and in the essential building blocks of community. Each component plays an essential role in neighbourhood formation. Each is mutually supportive. All are essential:

1. THE PLOT
All vernacular starts with the plot and its relationship with the building and the street; something we did very well in the past. Many of the successful models hinged around the narrow-fronted plot with the frontage dimension becoming the key indicator of wealth and social standing. Booth's Plan of London is a poverty map. It is also a map of plot frontages – the narrower the plot frontage, the lower the pecking order.

The plot is the smallest unit of mixed use and the smallest, and therefore, the most achievable unit of delivery. It provides an opportunity for independent timelines and introduces the possibility for individual responses – the preconditions for richness, variety and uniqueness. The plot only comes about through 'subdivision': The breaking up of the problem mountain into pebbles. The plot and building relationship has always been interdependent so we need to rediscover subdivision alongside the development of new building typologies. Many countries require plotting plans – some requiring very formal processes before development can happen. In Spain they call it an 'urbanizacion', in the new world, a 'township plan'. The problem with defining the plot as the only granular method is that it can become too limiting if its dimensions are fixed at the outset and cannot be easily changed. Of course, you could do what Tutti Frutti in Manchester did and release plots of land based on variable frontage dimensions. In other words if you only want six metres, you only buy six metres. This is like organic village growth. It works well for one-off, bespoke projects, but is less flexible for releasing larger chunks of land. It also does not readily facilitate regularities and default conditions, something that will be talked about extensively later in this book.

2. THE LOT
The lot is a parcel of land; a collection of plots. As a unit of subdivision it provides a more flexible way of breaking down the neighbourhood into smaller bits because it can be scaled up or down. We need to experiment with optimum lot, looking at the close relationship between:

- building typologies;

- design coding and guidance;

- delivery models; and

- development control.

The use of the lot gives us the first clue to setting potential default conditions that could give us ways of dealing with permitted development.

3. THE BLOCK

The block is the assembly of a number of plots or lots and provides an essential ordering device for districts, neighbourhoods and quarters. Efficient dimensioning and design of the block derives from a strong understanding of building typologies and their complex interrelationship with the street and plot. This is the reason why in places such as Cadogan Square in London or in the pattern of many Parisian blocks we see such successful urbanism. It is not just because of their great architecture, it is because these places demonstrate the efficiency that lies in a highly evolved urban solution. Street, plot, building and block become entwined – no waste, easily replicable.

Block design is an area of urban design theory and practice that has been overlooked in recent years – an understanding of the efficiency of the block in all its forms and its applications. Current urban design thinking sees the block as the consequence of the space left over and backfilled after the streets are defined by their desire lines; yet many great examples of planned urbanism show the block itself as a typological solution, none more so than the Victorians who built efficiently on a vast scale. If any criticism exists about Victorian city planning it lays in their limited application of different blocks and housing solutions in some towns and cities in Britain – a condition that often gets them accused of monotony, especially in those areas that have suffered housing market failure.

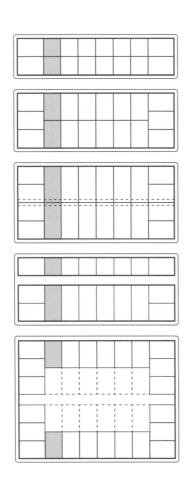

The block can take many forms from:

- The orthogonal linear or perimeter block with clearly defined back-to-back relationships.

- The soft centred block or superblock that can take later inner growth.

- The dual aspect block that has its frontage to the street and its service functions on a back lane.

- The mews block that has buildings separated from the street frontage buildings and accessed from a back lane. These mews could be under the same ownership as the frontage buildings or separate.

All of these are valid. All can accommodate a wide variety of typologies at various scales.

Block configurations showing the Lot.

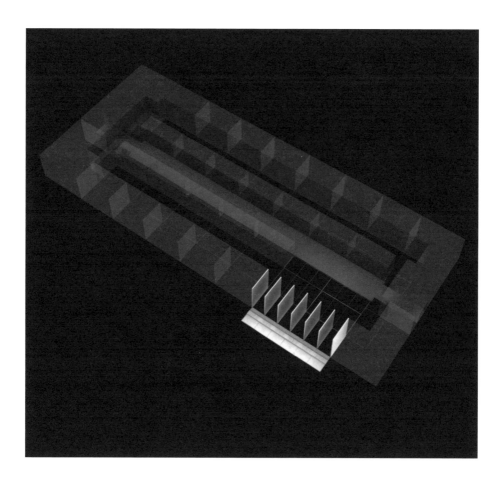

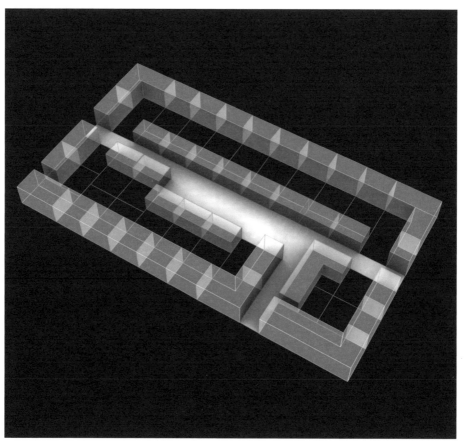

Mews and mews court block configurations showing the relationship of the lot to the plot

THE NEW NORM

The New Norm is an initiative we have developed through work on the proposed Newcastle Housing Expo. It is based on a methodology for parcelling development land into bite-size chunks using a progressive modular approach to enable: interchangeability, scalability, flexibility, and variety of response.

LOT-BASED URBANISM
As a fundamental concept the New Norm uses the 'Lot': a standard module of 15 metres wide as the basic unit of development. This can be subdivided into two, three or four plots or doubled and split into five plots as defined by common party walls. Along with the height of the building, these define the maximum building envelope and therefore the volume of each unit.

The 15 metre dimension was settled on after testing a range of lot dimensions with street and housing typologies. Detailed architectural testing by a panel of excellent architects and the results of many successful solutions from the Making the Popular Home architectural competition showed the robustness of the frontage dimension to accommodate the desired variety. By developing different dimensions to the depth of the block we could accommodate a wider range of building typologies. In this way we were structuring complex choices, retaining the benefits of the plot but still allowing greater flexibility with the lot.

With the 15 metre wide lot, we could, say:

- Use it as a single lot or subdivide it into four 3.75 metre; three 5 metre; or two 7.5 metre wide plots;

- Use two lots together to get three 10 metre; five 6 metre wide plots, or use them together to get a larger plot for say an apartment building; and

- Use variable dimensions within the widths of the one or two lot combinations.

These plot dimensions accommodated a wide range of housing and mixed-use building typologies from the mews cottage to the townhouse; living over the shop; the semi-detached to even the detached house. Our work on the London Mayor's Design Guide road-tested these dimensions against simple rules for apartment buildings, looking at optimum social dynamics within buildings, lengths of corridors and viability and found them to be remarkably robust.

Different internal and external layouts, garden design, type and façade can all be developed in adjacent units allowing architects to innovate. It enables internal growth and change within the concept of 'long life, loose fit'. It also allows for variation in street-scene and building shoulder height to create visual interest. The primary house or houses are aligned along the frontage of the plot, with various setback conditions.

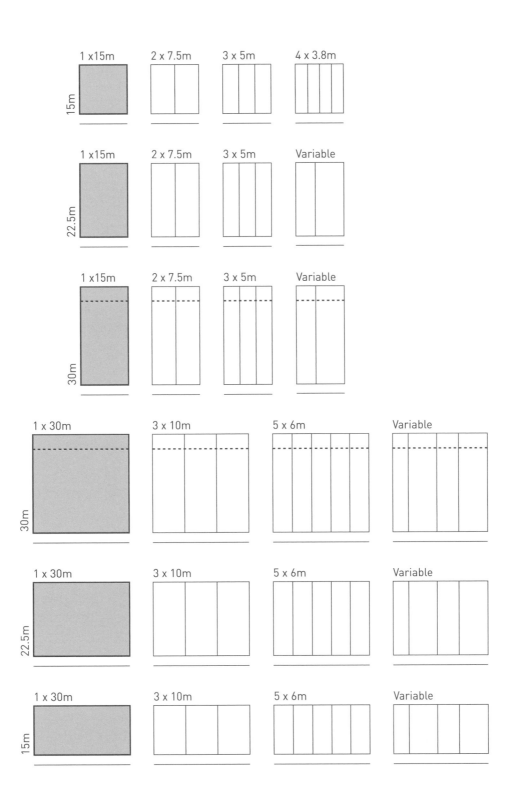

The New Norm identifies a number of different block typologies including the standard perimeter block, the mews perimeter block and the mews court perimeter block. These allow for different levels of intensification and a range of flexible uses to develop as part of a process of internal growth and change within the same site area. The New Norm proposes a hierarchy of street types based on the multi-functionality of the street as a critical part of the public realm. The subdivision plan provides an easy way of developing a regulating plan and guiding the production of simple design codes. As a result of this work we have used the principle of lot-based urbanism in a number of significant projects. The whole of the Aylesbury Estate in South London can be reduced to a 15 metre wide lot subdivision plan with full design codes. Three neighbourhood plans around the Stratford Olympics site are similar.

BAR CODE VS. DNA URBANISM

Now there are examples of new 'fine-grain' development in large modern developments and two examples spring to mind – Java Island in Amsterdam and Tutti Frutti in Manchester. The former is pre-programmed and therefore forced. In other words it is 'pretend variety' made to look interesting. The second is more responsive as it looks to richness and variety derived from the individual commissioning of design. Both use a 'bar-code' approach to achieving variety: In other words, for the sake of offering difference. There is nothing inherently wrong with this, but its total pursuit will just result in even more avant-garde: When everything is different it just becomes the same.

What we need is a DNA approach to achieving variety. This is the result of small and subtle shifts that are perfected over time and allow small individual responses. This is the way we treat our conservation areas and it raises the development of a contemporary vernacular that meets the needs of our society. The London Mayor's Housing Guide raised the need to look for a London vernacular, something that many European design approaches still favour: something that could evolve over time, something that is additive. Design for London refers to it as the 'new Georgian'. Group 91's work in 'Making of the Modern Street' in Dublin shows how collective architecture can lead to the development of something unique and timeless for a place. It is against the grain of the collective small that the special buildings can be reflected.

The 'bar code' approach at Java Island, Amsterdam

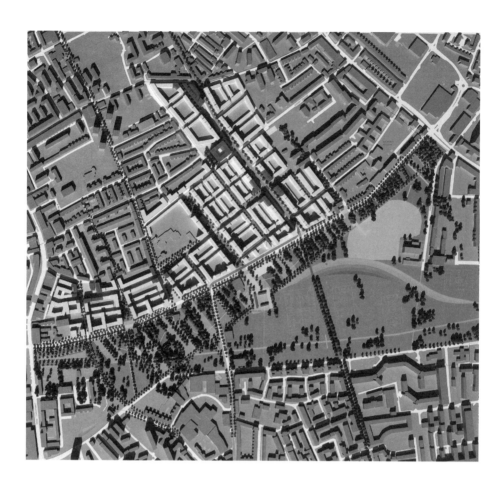

Top: Aylesbury Estate, South London: Lot-based urbanism applied
Bottom: 'The Making of the Modern Street', Group 91 Architects, Dublin

OPEN HIERARCHICAL PLAN-MAKING

If the plot, lot and block are the building blocks, how do you assemble these to make a neighbourhood? More importantly, how do you assemble these in an open hierarchical way to offer both regularity and perpetual novelty?

We have a long history of formal plan-making throughout civilisation that has served us well. A history where city blocks have been repetitively laid out in highly efficient patterns that reflect vernacular traditions and the higher order needs of the place and society. This tradition at a mass scale is best seen in the Roman 'castrum' plan whose standard, off-the-shelf imprint still exists in many European and North African towns and cities. The Roman grid is characterised by a near perfect orthogonal layout of streets, all crossing each other at right angles, and by the presence of two main streets, set at right angles from each other and called the 'cardo' and the 'decumanus'. At its intersection lies the 'forum', the heart of the place. In simple terms this is the main public space at the junction of two main roads, which gives us our networks. The urban blocks give us our fields.

Since then we have seen endless grids – formal, modified or distorted to suit the topography of the place (some even disregarding it) – produced on vellum or using Chinese inks in smoky plan-makers offices in government buildings or royal palaces. Rolled up, they have been dispatched to the surveyors to colonise the old and new world. These have given rise to the best and most enduring examples of planned urbanism we have ever seen:

- The nine-square grid plans of Jaipur based on ancient Hindu planning prin-ciples, later used by Balkrishna Doshi for its expansion a few decades ago;

- The Mediaeval bastides of southern France planned as fortified towns with a grid layout of intersecting streets, with wide thoroughfares that divide the town plan into insulae, or blocks, through which a narrow lane often runs, and a central market square surrounded by arcades (couverts) through which the axes of thoroughfares pass.

- In the Spanish colonisation of South America which saw King Phillip II's 'Laws of the Indes' specify the requirement for a square or rectangular central plaza with its eight principal streets running from the plaza's corners. Hundreds of grid-plan communities throughout the Americas were established according to this rigid pattern, echoing the practices of earlier Indian civilizations.

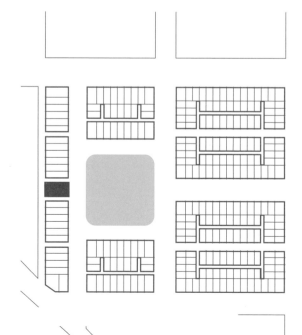

Edinburgh New Town

- The Portuguese downtown plans for Lisbon, rebuilt after the 1755 earthquake, largely according to the plans of the Marquess of Pombal. Instead of rebuilding the medieval town, Pombal decided to demolish the remains of the earthquake and rebuild the downtown in accordance with 'modern' urban rules. This plan with its rules was used as a template for Lourenco Marques in Mozambique and for many other Portuguese colonial settlements.

- The tradition of Scottish town-making with the formal grids of Inverary, Cullen, Stonehaven (well-illustrated in Tom Sharp's 'Anatomy of a Village') and the supergrid of Glasgow, which was the poster child for many North American and Canadian cities;

- The Victorian town plans that became standard fare for the colonisation of the Empire, where you can see the same DNA of the plan-maker in towns in Australia, New Zealand, Africa and the West Indies. All showed the same orthogonal approach with the town hall or church as the centrepiece to the town – urban blocks, lots and plots meticulously pegged out by the surveyors using chains.

- and so on......

OUR MOTHERBOARDS

Without doubt the two masterpieces of planned urbanism are the old world example of Edinburgh New Town and the new world Savannah in Georgia. Both demonstrate the idea of repetitive elements of streets and blocks, both are open and hierarchical. Both offer diversity within a logical framework

The former, planned by James Craig for the city fathers of Edinburgh, who were concerned about the poor health conditions in the old town, is a high point in Georgian rationalism in both architecture and planning. The latter laid out by General James Edward Oglethorpe in 1813 is remarkable.

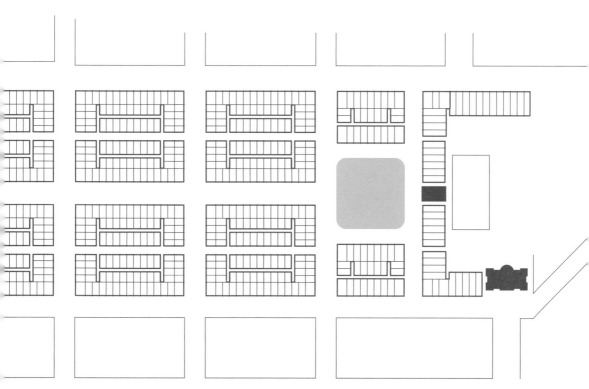

Savannah's hierarchically structured city plan is distinguished from those of previous colonial towns by its repeated pattern of connected neighbourhoods, multiple squares, streets, and designed expansion into lands held by the city (the common). It was the last colonial capital to be established by Britain in America. The basic plan unit is a ward, laid out with standard dimensions. Streets and building lots are organised around a central open space or square. Wards were originally organised as urban neighbourhoods with direct correlation to garden and farm lots in Oglethorpe's expanded regional plan system. The streets bounding the wards allow uninterrupted movement of traffic. Internal streets are interrupted by the squares to create a pedestrian-friendly scale that have adapted well over time. Savannah's plan reflects political and organisational considerations of the day. The repetitive egalitarian placement of wards, squares, and equal-sized lots points to the utopian ideals of the Quaker colony. The regularity of these lots controlled the size and rhythm of development to create a visually diverse and humanly scaled city.

Both demonstrate a remarkable robustness to accommodate new forms of living and working. Edinburgh New Town has adapted well to the flight of its banking industry to leafy business parks. Savannah has evolved into a place where each central square has taken on a different personality to reflect its surrounding land uses. They are both classically cities as a 'patterns in time'; like universal motherboards just waiting to process urban life.

More recently the Dutch have been showing us how to do it in places like Ijlburg in Holland. It is the sequence of the designer overlaying a standard repetitive grid plan on the site and trimming it to fit that is meaningful. We have always done this – dropping a plan on a context and modifying it to fit the vagaries of the place. The plan of Mayfair in London shows this where the legacy of the lost rivers of London are still reflected in narrow winding Marylebone Lane that break the formal grids. This introduces the delight of the unexpected. Nowhere is this delight more evident than in the plan of San Francisco which begs the question, 'Did the plan-makers ever visit the site?' Thank goodness they didn't, otherwise the car chases from 'Bullit' would never have been the same. The steep slopes of the San Francisco have modified the plan. The grid plan in turn has modified the place. Here, context is a modifier not a determinant. 'Push and push back', the essential conditions for emergence, have happened to the benefit of both sides.

Savannah, Georgia

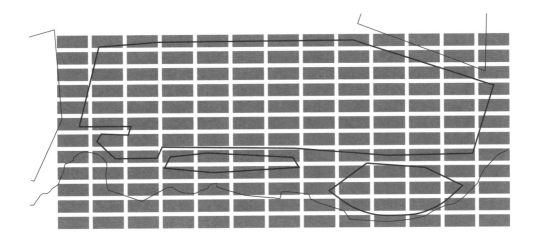

In Ijlburg you see the evolution of the trimmed plan to the modified grid and the new urban structure. Nothing complicated here: simplicity giving rise to complexity. So why are our urban designers making it so difficult? Why does everything have to start from first principles? If we are to offer anything to the evolution of our cities, towns and their districts, neighbourhoods and quarters we have to understand the tools of our craft better. Idle technocratic solutions or abstract clichés won't help. Looking to our past achievements and picking up the threads of this experience will. Plan-making is not difficult.

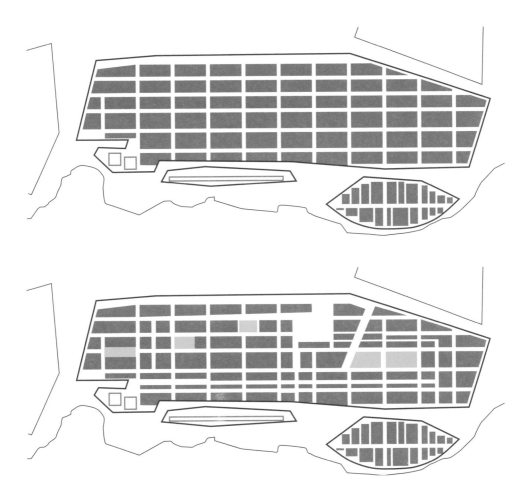

The evolution of the Ijlburg Masterplan

ACCRETION, CHOICE AND CHANGE

Understanding the initial design of a city is important but the first settlement within the land subdivisions is even more crucial, as the dominant process is the adjustment of block size and plot and lot dimensions to actual use. In general, the plot is more permanent than either the building or the street.

The grain of plots, set not by the original plan but by initial occupation and building on urban land, is perhaps the most enduring physical aspect of the city. Diversity begins in the process of early settlement. Still other diversity arises from accretion of new urban fabric.

Ways of facilitating this accretion, choice and progressive change include:

1. THE MIXED BAG METHOD

This means, like in Schumacher's concept of 'smallness in bigness', not everything needs to be small, but larger things should start from an agglomeration of the small. In other words, once we have a plot we can combine this into a lot, a block or even a whole phase of development, but we can always go back to the plot.

This has implication for land release from the smallest scale to larger chunks. In the default condition, agglomeration does not imply consolidation into larger chunks that allows the underlying fine grain to be lost. Where land is controlled by the public sector, combination of the elements allows different levels of entry and intervention by different players: individual, collective or corporate.

This method accommodates the full range of procurement options from individual self-build through to self-procurement; shell construction or full completion by any of a range of smaller local to larger contractors. For any scheme there should be a proportion of land given over to each and everyone of these activities, with the last option ideally being seen as a fallback position.

Local authorities could use parametric approaches to set and manage the percentage mix for each option and this could be monitored and adjusted based on relative success and take up of any option.

All of these procurement options should allow for the following:

- The individual building his own home operating at the plot scale;

- The collective, for example three individuals to purchase a lot for the development of a small scheme of three units;

- A local builder purchasing two lots to build five homes every year;

- A local housing association, who wish to build a small apartment building of no more than twenty units, to purchase two lots; and

- A national housebuilder who buys off plan, as their normal course of practice to keep their cash flow going, to purchase a whole phase of development comprising ten lots.

2. INNER GROWTH

The importance of the plot, lot and block relationship allows us to develop a number of methods to facilitate this process over time. This particular mechanism deliberately addresses the issue of accretion and evolutionary change. It gives rise to the potential for long-life, loose fit buildings to be delivered as needs change and for an increase in densities over time. It comes into play in the following way:

- The expansion of the building to allow for it to be vertically subdivided into smaller units;

- The long, deep plot or lot that allows access down the side for different forms of backland development;

- The mews block which allows for backland development to be separated with its own front door from the mews or lane;

- The soft-centred block that reserves the right for the introduction of a new lane or alley to allow access to infill development at the rear of the plot or lot. In this condition the soft centre is used for planting or shared recreation and takes on the qualities of a super-block.

Inner growth is an option that implies that the neighbourhood will be developed on a managed estate basis and is a good way for the estate to take out future receipts by allowing later development, much in the same way that the landlords in the large London estates manage their properties.

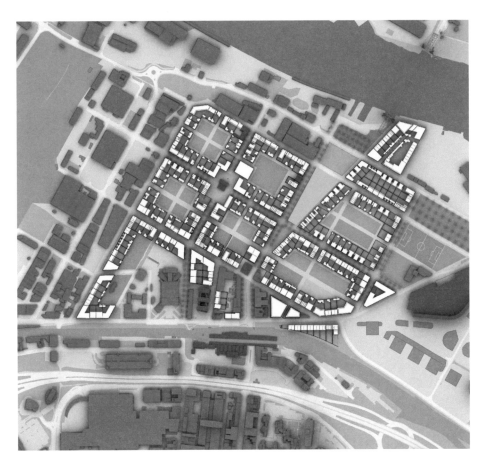

Middlehaven Plan, based on the original Quaker settlement and showing the use of the soft-centred block.

3. NEIGHBOURHOOD LAND DIVIDENDS

This mechanism overcomes the single formula offers that are the volume housebuilders' stock-in-trade. It applies in large urban extensions where the private sector is the only player. Rather than the full standard social housing contribution, an option could be framed to contribute a portion of the total land (say 10%), to the local authority or through say, a Community Land Trust. This would allow the Mixed Bag Method to be applied to this portion of land and introduce the necessary richness of mix and variety. The portion of land could be agreed in advance with the applicants or could be determined as a proportion of each phase. This means that if the housing market stalls, the local authority can still be experimenting with other forms of delivery.

4. SLOW LAND RELEASE METHOD

This method mediates the single big-bang approach to development and looks to open up more fronts in areas to allow incremental small change. As such, it is a way of local authorities hedging their bets. It could relate to careful phasing of schemes to ensure that we have progressive slow but continuous release of sites by a number of players, including the land captured through the Neighbourhood Land Dividend scheme. This will give local authorities a chance to monitor the effects of change, report on these and take different courses of action if necessary.

5. TARGET-DRIVEN CONSENTS

This method is a way preventing landbanking by linking planning consents to agreed delivery targets. In other words, if the housebuilder does not deliver on his agreed programme, the local authority can take various actions:

- someone else gets a chance to take up his target and, using the Slow Land Release principle, they are phased later;

- the local authority can chose to increase their share of the total land consented to boost their Neighbourhood Land Dividend; or consent lapses.

Each of these options should be trialled. The first three have already been tested against established practices and policy constraints and may not be difficult to implement. They just require considered thinking.

WHAT ARE THE NEW BEHAVIOURS?

All of the above mechanisms require a fundamental shift in behaviour in planning, design and delivery, some more radical than others

A. FOR PLANNING

Many of the mechanisms identified in this section can be delivered through the planning system at present. Others may require primary legislation that could be introduced through the Localism Bill. Assuming some form of 'urban structure plan' is in place, the most significant new departure will be the use of plot or lot plans in combination with innovative land release strategies. Using local development orders in association with subdivision plans enables us to deliver more effective design codes. These could be extended to new proposals for Neighbourhood Development Orders or even Residential Planning Zones, as we find in other parts of the world. With these in place, planning becomes real planning. Control devolves to the lowest level. Monitoring and feedback become the new behaviour.

B. FOR DESIGN

This means developing more and constantly evolving typological solutions tailored to and informing the specific requirements of the plot and lot within its context. Choice is opened to a wider range of players. Everyone is happy.

C. FOR DELIVERY

This is where the most radical shift in behaviour is needed, particularly for publicly owned land where we need to move away from large scale release to smaller lots. It also has a major impact on major private owned sites, where the neighbourhood land dividend will impact on the housebuilder. This would require careful testing.

In all the land release options everyone has a bite of the apple. Timelines are independent. Complex choices can be made. Massive small change can happen.

DEFAULT [noun]: *choice or setting that applies in the absence of active intervention*

CONDITION 4:
SET STANDARD DEFAULTS

Defaults are standard settings or choices that apply to individuals who do not take active steps to change them. They are a soft way of influencing positive choices, where development is more likely to turn out in a way proven to make good urbanism work from past experience. Using defaults also implies that if you do not like the standard setting you can personalise it.

Behavioural scientists attribute this to the 'status quo –bias'; the common human resistance to changing one's behaviour, combined with another common phenomenon: the tendency to conform. Nowhere is this more so than in housing choice, and this is what has driven the housebuilder's products over the years. There is a counter to this, however. Most people can only buy what is on offer.

So the real questions are:

- what choices are available?

- what are the pathways to this choice?

- having made it, how do I procure it?

- what guides me?

These questions give rise to something more fundamental. What is the standard offer and if I don't like it, how can I modify it or do something completely different?

THE NATURE OF CONFORMITY

Behavioural research by Everett Rogers into the 'tipping point' in adopting new ideas has shown that when given choice, most people tend to adopt the new offer once early innovation has been accepted by the early adopters. If you look at Rogers' bell curve, it explains this preponderance of conformity. The largest number of adopters of any process is the early and late majority and the 'laggards', accounting for well over 80% of the total.

According to Rogers, the 'Early Majority' – accounting for some 34% of the total – rather than looking for revolutionary changes, are motivated by evolutionary changes. They have three principles they follow:

- When it is time to move, let's move all together.

- When we pick an innovation to lead us to the new paradigm, let us all pick the same one.

- Once the transition starts, the sooner we get it over with, the better.

In the absence of continuous innovation, it is this group that the housebuilders fail to mobilise effectively. They are the group who will stabilise the next default settings.

The next 34% of adopters are the 'Late Majority'. They are sceptical, traditional and are very price sensitive and require completely pre-assembled, bulletproof solutions. They are the classic conformers that the default settings apply to. The last 16% of the adopters consists of 'Laggards'. Laggards are sceptics who want only to maintain the status quo.

If you apply these statistics to bottom-up neighbourhood formation it shows that developing the quality and content of the standard offer, once you have triggered innovation, will have a far greater impact than any other single factor in delivering successful places.

STATED PREFERENCES

The Localism Bill gives the potential for local design guidance where communities determine what they like or dislike, a condition that has many designers squirming. CABE's report 'What Home Buyers Want' throws up many unsurprising facts. The survey by Mulholland Research and Consulting shows that most people want to live in somewhere distinctive and with character – which is often expressed as a preference for old buildings rather than new. But it is richer architecture that is wanted, and bland 'traditional' is unpopular along with minimal modernism. Individuality was desirable, within limits – a home should look similar but not the same as others in the vicinity.

Localism places more emphasis on local communities' stated preferences. This places more emphasis on designers to innovate within these constraints.

TOWARDS A NEW VERNACULAR

There is also nothing wrong with the standard offer. We have being using it for years. We call it the 'norm' – a standard or model or pattern regarded as typical – and most societies have evolved their responses to doing things in a normal way. Most of the cities we love have these qualities, as Monocle magazine shows in its Liveable Cities Index. In housing we call it the 'Popular Home'. In urbanism we call it 'vernacular' and we can take inspiration from it.

The formal characteristics of both vernacular urban patterns and housing appear as a consequence of well determined needs, easily coping with the demand of social, cultural and functional changes through the process of easy adaptability – which is the basic issue of sustainable urban living.

The London Housing Design Guide aspires to encourage a new London vernacular that can take its place in this rich fabric. A new vernacular does not propose a singular architectural style, but recognises that the best housing comes from robust guidelines in planning and regulation, together with a deep understanding of particular architectural and social contexts on the part of designers and developers.

—Boris Johnson, Mayor of London

In our work on the Mayor of London's Housing Design Guide we showed that in the last half of the 20th century the collective urban identity and legibility of London's housing was lost. Much recent housing has been incoherent and arbitrary. However, a study of London's historical housing is a study of London's vernacular. From the Georgian terraces of Islington to the Edwardian mansion blocks of Bloomsbury and the Victorian semis of Clapham, London has always had its own vernacular. This tends to evolve over time to reflect the environmental, cultural and historical context in which it exists. It's not a style but the way buildings are put together in a given region. Vernacular architecture is of its place and specifically adapted to its site addressing issues of climate, orientation and aspect. It is of its time, employing direct methods of construction using locally available resources and being authentic in its use of materials. Vernacular housing tends to have typological clarity that is lacking in much recent development.

It should not be confused with historicist styling. CABE's Housing Audit simultaneously criticised the lack of vernacular design at the same time as warning of "the heavy-handed and superficial application of general "historicist" or "rural style". The Essex Design Guide and Poundbury may have a lot to do with this fictionalising of vernacular. New housing that favours laconic, background architecture would offer coherence to our developing neighbourhoods and provide respite from the flashy, self-promoting, placeless architecture that sees every site as a landmark opportunity.

The real problem is that 'vernacular' which is an ever changing and self-perfecting process has stalled. Monopolistic practices in the control of land and delivery of housing in Britain has given us a 'one-trick pony' and the challenge lies in how we can drive up choice and quality of the standard offer without just using the same old 'better design' story.

Mark Parsons in his paper 'Towards a New Vernacular' argues that he has less of an issue with the space standards that housebuilders are providing. In contrast, housing layouts, their street size and form, their public open spaces and the space between dwellings are imposed by government regulation. Highway and pavement widths, turning and car parking requirements, and the cul-de-sac layout produces a suburban form or 'estatescape' of isolated architectural elements. The houses drown in 'a sea' of minimum widths and minimum standards. Add to this the planning requirements of minimum distance and minimum space and you have it. The contemporary housing estate built as a cell unrelated to its surrounds. He says,

> *Vernacular is relevant to our own time. The principles often prescribed to historic vernacular architecture are those that are generally applied, today, to the meaning of sustainability. Buildings of simple quality, reusable and adaptable, produced from materials that are freely available and economic to produce and use in construction. The historic architectural vernacular was created by the 'pressures' of their time; the availability of construction materials and land; the cost of transporting and processing those materials into their required form; and the availability and cost of the craft skills necessary to put them together.*
>
> *Some of these 'pressures' should be re-imposed. Not by strict regulation of design or by trying to manipulate or impose a particular architectural 'taste', but by controlling the availability and source of construction materials. This could be achieved through offering tax and financial incentives for local sourcing, reusing materials and buying those which are both energy efficient and renewable; encouraging a move away from employment taxation towards taxation which targets construction materials which require large doses of nonrenewable and polluting energy (the cost of labour more than anything else prevents the development of good building art and craft). This together with an emphasis on localised government; the provision of smaller housing estates; changes in highway design; and a rethinking of spacing standards; could achieve more intimacy, a scale more in keeping with people and which we could happily live with, made up of houses which are truly distinctive and of their place and time. The new vernacular housing may well be very different.*

What we do need is a vernacular that is relevant to our own time: a 'new norm'. This is something we have being trialling in our work on the 'Reinventing the Popular Home' in recent years: work that was taken forward in the London Mayor's Housing Design Guide.

ROLE OF STANDARDS

Standards should not be confused with defaults. Standards are written definitions, limits, or rules, approved and monitored for compliance by authoritative agencies or recognised bodies as minimum acceptable benchmarks. The standard offer should also not be confused with standards, although there is some linkage. Space standards are the eternal conundrum and, in a world where we are looking for long-life loose fit solutions, do they apply? It is true that with monopolistic practices the standard product has driven down the size of rooms. Boris Johnson calls this "Rabbit hutch Britain", but does this define the need for minimum space standards? If there was just more choice, this might be ironed out.

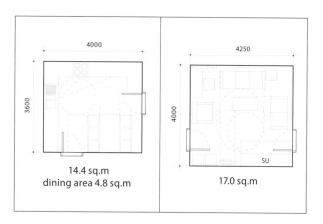

Parker Morris was a means of giving the housing industry some fixes, but is it still valid in a rapidly changing social and cultural environment where all requirements can be reduced to two-point-four person households. Families have moved on. We now have complexity in all its forms. If we rather moved to the quality of overall space criteria (and volume) as a universal choice rather than specific requirements for every room, we could open up choice as to how people used their space. It they chose to have smaller bedrooms and trade this off against larger living space, so what? One thing we have shown in our more robust housing forms, interiors can change.

Standards help frame or qualify standard offers, they should not determine them. In other words they can show that places will accommodate certain uses, they do not need to be the only way they are achieved. Some of our best conservation areas do not readily accommodate all the mechanics of ideal modern operating. Some of our best starter housing is in small houses designed for workers living that break all the normal space standard rules. The more limiting nature of our housing standards lies in Lifetime Homes requirements. If we applied these to the letter of the law then we would never be able to deliver the robust type of housing that the conversion of Victorian housing has given us in recent years.

In a 'vernacular' world the home evolves to the pattern of living at the time. It is not phrased by narrow limiting rules.

TYPOLOGICAL SOLUTIONS

Typology is the classification of (usually physical) characteristics commonly found in buildings and urban places, according to their association with different categories, such as intensity of development (from natural or rural to highly urban), degrees of formality, and school of thought (for example, modernist or traditional). Individual characteristics form patterns.

Patterns relate elements hierarchically across physical scales (from small details to large systems). An emphasis on typology is important to match the physical development characteristics of a place within the appropriate typology for that place, as determined by local preferences taken in context with urban patterns as evidenced throughout history.

Places are defined by their building typologies, the London townhouse, the New York tram house, the Amsterdam canal house, the Tyneside flat and the Glasgow tenement. They are also defined by their patterns of development, which are also typological, the London garden squares; the Edinburgh burgages and the Beijing hutongs.

The housebuilders use a palette of typologies... but, badly. The main problem is that they are generally influenced by the need to keep the planners happy, based on loose and ill-formed constructs of character and distinctiveness. In doing so they become characterless and indistinctive. Designers would do well to work on evolving a range of typologies suitable to the requirements of a place. The housebuilders just need a new palette as their default options.

In recent years we have seen the proliferation of two dominant housing models: high density apartment living and low density houses that derive largely from suburban traditions. The high-density model has salved our conscience on sustainability but has not had given us well-balanced communities, many having the exact opposite effect. We now need to focus more on developing effective medium density typologies similar to those in the best parts of many of our cities. This recognises that these are best suited to achieve sufficient densities for sustainable development and still give us the critical mass and intensity for strong neighbourhood formation.

Bedford Square - the Georgian 'posterchild' for typological solutions

PATTERN BOOKS

The pattern book has a long and architecturally respectable history, but they tend to be frowned upon by architects, who see them as a threat to the profession. Significantly, pattern books were the stuff of the building trade in the centuries before architects were professionalised. There was Palladio's Quattro Libri (1570), Colen Campbell's Vitruvius Britannicus (1715), Batty and Thomas Langley's City and Country Builder's and Workman's Treasury of Design (1740) and JC Loudon's The Encyclopaedia of Cottage, Farm, Villa Architecture (1834). These all provided templates for builders, creating not uniformity but consistency. Even more significantly, these pattern books were the inspiration for Georgian urbanism. The old 1978 Greater London Council's 'An Introduction to Housing Layout' was a source of inspiration for many looking for standard house plans. Since then we appear to have very little typological research other than that we can glean from our Dutch and German counterparts, who still see typology as a valid pursuit.

In the matter of putting quality back into housing, Pierre d'Avoine, who advocates, in his persuasive book Housey, Housey (Black Dog, 2005), a return to pattern books. D'Avoine is not advocating servile copyism, but a radical reinterpretation of the idea. If design is to replace dogma, that includes modernist dogma, too. The fundamental idea behind the pattern book is a reproducible formula, which can be shaped to suit different, needs, be they physical, economic or cultural. There is a great opportunity, therefore, to introduce into the housing supply a greater range of choice, by instituting new procedures of developing land in smaller parcels, on a more individual basis, using standardised construction methods which can nevertheless deliver 'desirability' and accommodation suitable for today's lifestyles, within a plausible budget.

As regards affordability, Alex Eley, who co-authored the London Mayor's Design Guide with Urban Initiatives, pointed out that in 2006, in the English Partnerships Design for Manufacture initiative, which aimed to create a sustainable home for £60,000, the homes delivered offered an average of 76 square metres of living space for the £60,000. Other 'pattern book' homes, for example the German Hebel Haus, deliver 108 square metres, with three bedrooms, for £47,800.

Pattern book housing is something the Americans have been doing for years with such products as the Sears House. Some companies specialise in particular housing solutions for specific markets – one company only providing modular workers housing on miniature lots measuring 5 metres wide. Working in modular dimensions shows us that you can live well in small spaces, and buildings designed in this manner can be organised to fit a variety of situations and can be configured to solve issues of site, orientation, needs, and desires.

Work on plot, lot and block-based urbanism shows us the importance of modular dimensions and their ability to spawn a number of permutations. The Popular Home initiative also shows that we can build pattern books that offer the widest range of choice that can be applied to default settings.

OPEN BUILDING

We all know that most ordinary buildings change in large and small ways to remain useful. We also know that, in general, the best buildings are those most able to provide capacity to changing functions, standards of use and life-style, and improved parts over time. John Habraken first articulated the principles of Open Building in his book 'Supports'. He argued that housing must always recognise two domains of action–the action of the community and that of the individual inhabitant. When the inhabitant is excluded, the result is uniformity and rigidity. When only the individual takes action, the result may be chaos and conflict. This formulation of a necessary balance of control had implications for all parties in the housing process.

Open building is the term used to indicate a number of different but related ideas about universal solutions for making of environments. These include:

- The idea of distinct levels of intervention in the built environment, such as those represented by the base building and the fitout, or by urban design and architecture.

- The idea that users or inhabitants may make design decisions as well as urban professionals.

- The idea that, more generally, designing is a process with multiple participants also including different kinds of professionals.

- The idea that the interface between technical systems allows the replacement of one system with another performing the same function.

- The idea that built environment is in constant transformation and change must be recognised and understood.

- The idea that built environment is the product of an ongoing, never ending design process, in which environment transforms part by part.

Those who subscribe to the Open Building approach seek to formulate theories about the built environment seen in this dynamic way and to develop methods of design and building construction that are compatible with it.

Open building is also a pragmatic answer to a state of technical entanglement in buildings that has resulted from the incremental addition, over a long period of time, of new technical systems and the "ownership" of these new systems by different trades who rarely cooperate. These pressures are forcing all parties to reconsider and realign their procurement and investment practices, their design methods, and their regulatory systems.

These changes in attitude and priorities are taking the force of law. In 2008 the Japanese parliament passed new laws mandating 200 year housing, accompanying the legislation with a set of regulatory and administrative tools for use by local building officials who have the responsibility to evaluate and approve building projects. Projects approved under the new law receive a reduced rate of taxation. In Finland, one of the largest real estate companies develops open building projects for their residential portfolio. In the Netherlands, a number of companies–from product manufacturers to developers to architects–implement open building by other names. In Poland open building is known as the "Warsaw Standard".

'Shell and core' buildings are an expression of principles of open building. This is where the contractor moves to the next level by providing the full enclosure of the home with service connections and stair and lift cores. This allows for the individual to configure and fit out their own internal spaces.

STARTER PACKS

There is another part-build solution that lies between serviced sites and 'shell and core' and it involves the standardisation and modularisation of the most basic primary structure of the building, which can be delivered most effectively through mass housing or large construction methods. In terraced development it can be reduced to the 'universal party walls' and apartment buildings it is the cellular structure of wall and slabs: the 'urban warehouse' concept. These are the elements of the building that should never need to change, no matter how much the building is adapted over the years. Everything else should be changeable.

These elements are also important because they address the most difficult concerns of the self-builder or small builder: setting the bounds of the project, limiting choice and starting up. These elements define the boundaries of the site, and therefore relationship and extent with adjacent sites. They are a major determinant in defining the volume of the building by also defining the conditions for the front and back solutions. They also provide the essential structure that allows more domestic and traditional forms of structure to be utilised for roofs and internal walls and floors, all of which that can be easily changed. In both instances the contractor can proceed to the next level of part-build: shell-and-core, which allows for internal fitout by the occupants.

So what we need now is a new breed of 'enabling' contractor (who do not want to become the developer) to meet this challenge. They exist in abundance in other parts of Europe. We are surprised they don't exist here.

1. UNIVERSAL PARTY WALLS

We need to develop party wall construction methods that use the benefits of mass construction but still facilitate traditional response. Something that offers speed, consistency and regularity. They can be delivered using proprietary methods or conventional construction but they must all have the same outcome: delivering volume of space. In order to achieve this party walls need an element of modularity using standard heights and lengths for a range of medium housing density conditions. We can learn a lot about this approach from kitchen design, which has standard sets of dimensions for its cabinets – tall and short, wide and narrow – that have become universal. If you don't like the standard items you can fit your own doors, tops or appliances. Stoves, dishwashers and fridges all fit! Choice is well structured.

If the carcass of the cabinet fixes the volume, where you choose to fix the height and number of the shelves is your choice, and this might change. In a similar way the party walls, in defining the volume of the building, should offer different internal responses. We know that most floors are fixed to deliver minimum floor to ceiling heights but what happens if we choose to trade off volume for floorspace? We just need the equivalent of the lug holes in the kitchen cabinet that offers simple choice.

The Newcastle Housing Expo gave us a chance to test these ideas against space standards, modern methods of construction and industry practice in other parts of Europe. It is not difficult to do if we put our mind to it!

FIX

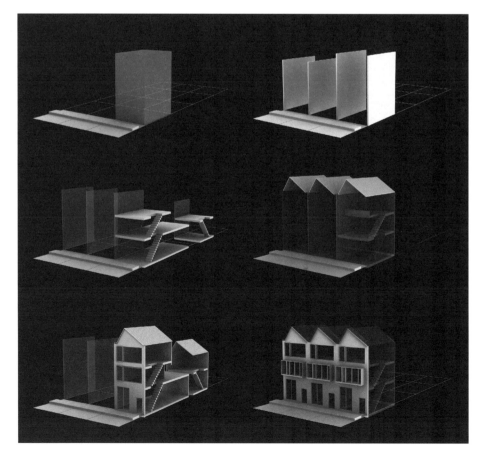

Party walls as the main definer of volume in Newcastle Expo.

2. THE URBAN WAREHOUSE

If the standard Victorian warehouse is one of the most robust forms of urban building that can accommodate the widest range of uses, why do we not just build more of these and allow people to fit them out, if they want?

Alex Lipschutz has been working with engineers ARUP, to develop a system that can provide sustainable, adaptable structures that will last the test of time – the modern version of the urban warehouse. The recently prototyped system has an efficient storey height that is only slightly taller than that normal for residential buildings but well inside standard office dimensions. This generates a floor to ceiling height accommodating, offices, shops, restaurants and generous residential units of all types (hotel, student housing, affordable, market and loft flats). The system can support the highest loads for offices and therefore easily cope with housing of all kinds. The floor is fully accessible for services and deep enough to permit offices above apartments and vice versa so that uses can be exchanged within and between buildings. Most importantly, the structure uses a minimum amount of material, can be recycled and encourages a green environmental system that utilises free night cooling. It is a classic open, long-life, loose-fit solution.

We need more thinking like this, getting us away from our obsession with single use, form-based architecture that has not served us well. Like Japan, Holland and Poland we should be moving towards 200 year buildings that come with effective regulatory tools and with generous tax incentives.

Cranfield Mills, Ipswich – a Victorian warehouse with a new life

DESIGN CODES

A design code is a set of specific rules or requirements to guide the physical development of a site or place. The aim of design coding is to provide clarity as to what constitutes acceptable design quality and thereby a level of certainty for developers and the local community alike that can help to facilitate the delivery of good quality new development.

A criticism commonly levelled at the use of design codes is that while they may help to determine the minimum acceptable standards of design, codes do little to encourage innovative architecture. In contrast, Carmona and Dann (2007) suggest design codes may encourage innovation through the appointment of better quality designers since they help to raise the profile of design from the outset. They also find that design codes can raise design quality by challenging traditional development processes, particularly in relation to house building. A design code may be used with a Local Development Order (LDO) by a local planning authority to extend permitted development rights and aid the speedy delivery of developments while retaining high quality design content.

All stakeholders have the potential to benefit from the use of an LDO. Local authorities that choose to use an LDO with design codes have the additional benefits over and above the standard permitted development rights, with the option of prescribing 'must haves' (for example road widths and building heights) and allowing some leeway for meeting requirements where the principle must be met. Once the LDO was set up, the developer would be able to progress with greater speed and certainty, providing the scheme is compliant with the design code and the terms of the conditions of the Order.

One of the issues associated with design codes are that locally accepted typological solutions are often not available. This means therefore that there are ever-demanding pressures to return to first principles. Many aspects of development – street typologies, block patterns, open space solutions and subdivision principles – could be dealt with as neighbourhood wide (or even city wide) development orders. This would work with the new government's announcement on Neighbourhood Development Orders. Design codes may be a tool for large-scale development but if we were looking to diversify the housebuilding industry and promote more local interventions, they would need to be evolved as a mechanism to guide small scale self-build or self-procured developments. By using Neighbourhood Development Orders, there is no reason why local authorities could not adopt a borough-wide pattern book approach, offering a range of typological housing solutions that could be used off-the-shelf as default settings.

If you adopt the Plot<Lot>Block approach, the scheme almost becomes self-regulating and simple rules can be used to ensure richness and variety. The design code for Borneo Sporenburg in Amsterdam, an example of fine-grain development, is written on a single side of paper. The Aylesbury Estate in South London has followed a similar approach with a design code linked to plot and lot configurations.

THE POPULAR HOME

The Popular Home is an initiative that closely builds on the plot, lot and block subdivision principles described earlier. It looks to making long life, loose fit housing as an essential component of compact neighbourhoods and as a common sense alternative to the outdated models that populate the national housebuilding industry today.

It sets a new benchmark for our housing challenge, ensuring the best possible outcomes in medium density housing design, neighbourhood building and long term management and maintenance, through a restatement of underlying values, through a clarity of purpose and through a pioneering approach to innovation:

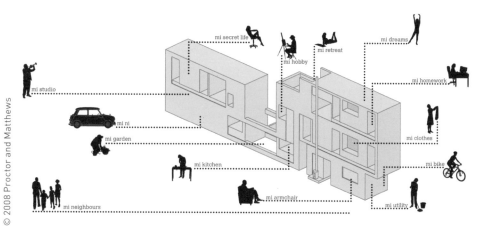

FIX

- It embraces the needs of a complex and changing society recognising the rapidly changing social and demographic changes in society that shape new forms of urban living, social patterns and lifetime requirements and poses new models of design, delivery and management for new housing.

- It imbeds environmentalism as an integrated design requirement by promoting efficient use of land and taking the lead in innovative environmental design of new housing, avoiding unnecessary 'eco-clichés' and making a real difference to sustainable building and urban design.

- It recognises the importance of building communities and explores the potential for making them well-balanced through a range of social actions, management projects and programmes to foster early sense of belonging in a community and build long-term stability in a community.

- It searches for new housing models by exploring a new planning, design and delivery approach to buildings in the context of the plot, lot and block by promoting a flexible typological approach to these scales of development and combining the advantages of modern methods of construction with the benefits of repetition, rhythm and harmony that evolve from the traditions of good housing and urban design.

- It looks to new ways of disseminating and influencing choice by developing 'pattern book' approaches to building design: allowing for easy interchangeability of units; use of modular dimensions, systems and practices; easy modification and tailoring to the specific needs of a place.

Above: The 'mi home' by Proctor and Mathews is a reinterpretation of the terraced house; Overleaf: Our emerging pattern book.

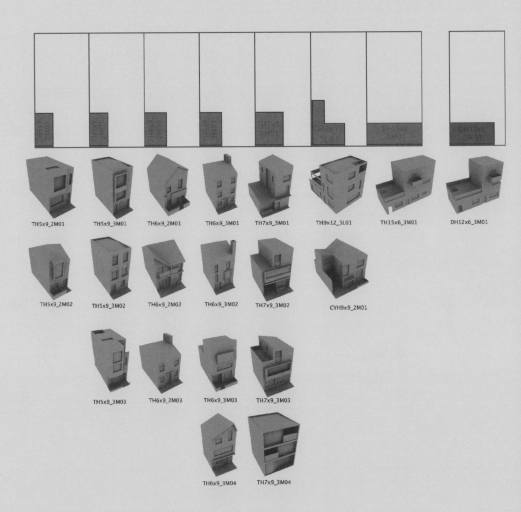

TH5x9_2M01 TH5x9_3M01 TH6x9_2M01 TH6x9_3M01 TH7x9_3M01 TH9x12_3L01 TH15x6_3M01 DH12x6_3M01

TH5x9_2M02 TH5x9_3M02 TH6x9_2M02 TH6x9_3M02 TH7x9_3M02 CYH9x9_2M01

TH5x9_3M03 TH6x9_2M03 TH6x9_3M03 TH7x9_3M03

TH6x9_3M04 TH7x9_3M04

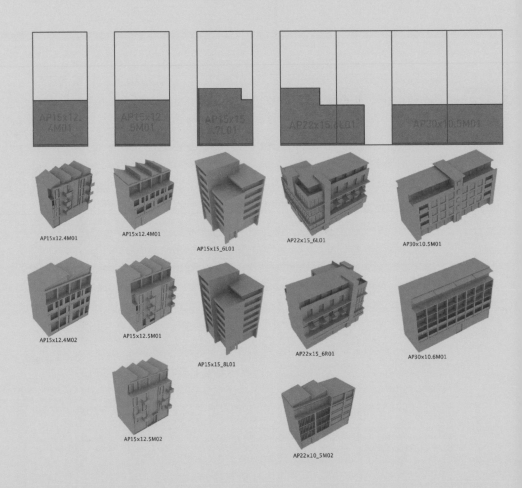

AP15x12.4M01 AP15x12.4M01

AP15x15_6L01

AP22x15_6L01

AP30x10.5M01

AP15x12.4M02 AP15x12.5M01

AP15x15_8L01

AP22x15_6R01

AP30x10.6M01

AP15x12.5M02

AP22x10_5M02

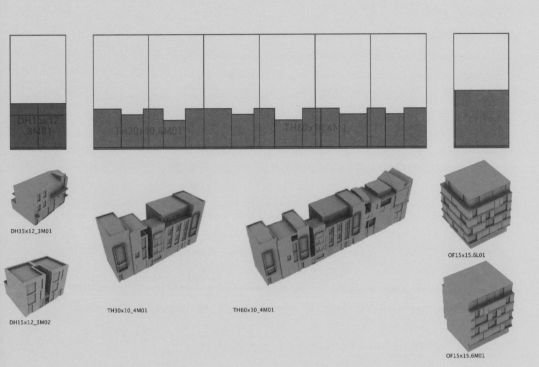

DH15x12_3M01

DH15x12_3M02

TH30x10_4M01

TH60x10_4M01

OF15x15.6L01

OF15x15.6M01

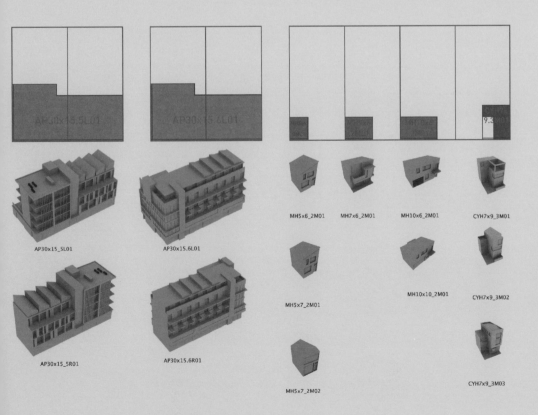

AP30x15_5L01

AP30x15.6L01

AP30x15_5R01

AP30x15.6R01

MH5x6_2M01

MH7x6_2M01

MH10x6_2M01

CYH7x9_3M01

MH5x7_2M01

MH10x10_2M01

CYH7x9_3M02

MH5x7_2M02

CYH7x9_3M03

TESTING THE LOT CONCEPT

Using the Universal Party Wall and Urban Warehouse approach, the Popular Home Initiative allows for the sourcing of common modules or parts to ensure quality and reduce build costs and complexities. It enables units to be developed to different specifications and even levels of completion, whilst still using a common 'kit of parts' for each of the key modules of a house – allowing for standardisation to ease building and achieve economies of scale. Initial work by a panel of architects looked at testing lot configurations to see if any logical patterns emerged and, if so, could we develop house types as a number of interchangeable parts in the plan.

As stated previously, the 15 metre lot proved to be the most versatile and efficient as a dimension in accommodating many robust plan types for party wall solutions, whilst also offering the potential to be used in pairs to accommodate the urban warehouse typologies. The project moved forward on this basis. Working within the constraints of the 15 metre wide lot, the architects developed a range of house types using party wall dimensions as narrow as 3.75 metres with others of 5, 6, 7.5 and 10 metres wide, accepting that two lots could be combined to give greater variation. These included narrow and wide fronted typologies for:

- Mews and studio units for live/work use on back lanes.

- Terraced housing solutions including two and three storey options with the potential for loft conversions.

- Semi-detached housing and free-standing urban villas.

- House-over house-options and live-work units.

- Apartment and living-over-the-shop solutions

The project also recognised that we could use variable dimensions within the widths of the one or two lot combinations to allow for more bespoke solutions.

The volumetric/plot width normative approach allows for huge variation in architecture and house types, fully tested by our architect panel, but with sufficient standards to ensure that the place still works in urban design terms. It also lends itself to being effectively coded and simple rules to be written to achieve richness and variety within regularity.

This work led to an invited design competition being run by the Royal Institute of British Architects (RIBA) Competitions Office, in association with Newcastle City Council and English Partnerships.

FIX

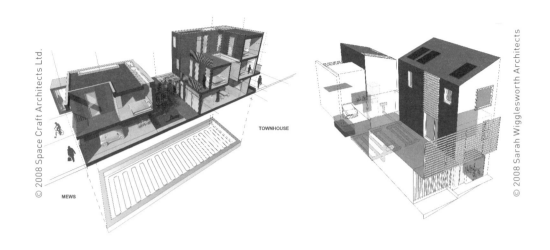

TOWNHOUSE

MEWS

FIX

Top left: "Lifetime cycle" by Space Craft;
Top right: "Flip Flop Flex House" by Sarah Wigglesworth;
Middle: "The Courtyard Dwelling" by JM Architects;
Bottom: "Lifetime cycle" by Space Craft

ALTERNATIVE PROCUREMENT MODELS

There is a predominant business model in the classic British housebuilder, encompassing all phases of the housebuilding process and selling onto a general market. But the crisis in the British housebuilding industry could result in significant changes to the way new properties are financed, built and planned, according to a 2009 report 'The Future of Residential Development' by Knight Frank. The report also highlights that the public sector has an increasing role in the land market. With government agencies and housing associations representing a large chunk of purchasers, they are almost as active as private investors. The consequence could be that traditional volume housebuilders could play a smaller role in the delivery of homes in the future.

Another avenue through which housing is provided is through self-build or self-procurement of housing by the final occupant. Self-build occurs when a prospective homeowner buys a plot of land and builds a dwelling. The actual amount of self-building undertaken varies as architects and other professionals are typically used and builders may be hired to undertake part or all of the works. But in all cases, the self-builder takes on key development risks. They include raising the finance, acquiring the land, applying for planning permission, deciding on designs, opting for building methods and standards, and choosing the final dwelling fit-out.

The Department of Communities and Local Government (DCLG) report 'The Housebuilding Industry: Promoting Recovery in Housing Supply' recognises that expanding housing supply is a priority for government. It has been known for some years that housing shortages are now intensifying and growing. The output of the housebuilding industry has shrunk by a half and it is not easy to turn it back on as resources, capital and confidence have been lost. One of its key recommendations of this report is promoting diversity of provision. Diversity does not happen by chance but is a result of the nature of housebuilding, entrepreneurship and competition, and of the environments in which they exist. Diversity of provision offers benefits to consumers in a wider range of product choice, including self-build. More than 55% of housing in Germany is created using self-build or self-procurement techniques, 45% in France, and as little as 3-4% in Britain. This opens up the opportunity for a significant increase in self-build.

There are a number of significant benefits that flow from this approach. For a residential self-builder this could be as simple as a place to live, which is designed and specified to meet his/her own requirements. For a commercial occupier, a bespoke design might project a certain image or achieve efficiencies that improve the profitability of the business. In both cases, the benefits go beyond those that would be considered by a developer who looks only at the property. Self build can also allow a different perspective on developers profit. By taking out the 'middle man', profit on costs of 10-25% can be taken out of the appraisal moving it towards financial viability. Some construction work can be undertaken by the self builder to further reduce costs and the need for borrowing.

It also encourages entrants that may have innovative ideas in terms of design, building methods or consumer service. It improves competition within the industry and helps to ensure that smaller types of sites are developed. Diversity of provision should be supported but only to ensure a level playing field. Sweat equity, also called community self-build, is a term used to describe the contribution made to a project by people who contribute their time and effort. Community-based self-build projects took off in Bristol in the mid-1980s, which helped unemployed builders into work. More than 120 schemes, have since been completed, providing 1,000 homes. Depending on the scheme, community self-builders assume outright ownership, part ownership or the right to low-cost rent in return for their labour.

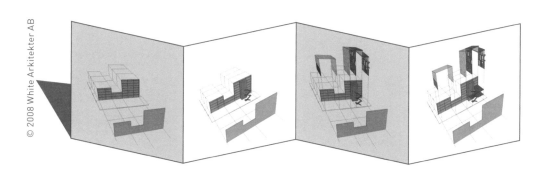

STRUCTURING COMPLEX CHOICES

The move to Localism and the recently announced Community Right to Build programme will have a significant effect on the need to diversify provision and all of the alternative routes to procurement will take on more importance. We can assume that bottom-up will widen choice as systems become more open. This could lead to confusion as each community experiments with its own ideas or we can choose to help them with their default choices. These choices are conditioned by four factors:

TYPE OF ACTION
As shown in the Mixed Bag Method in Condition 2: FIELDS there are three types of agents who can be involved in building for neighbourhood formation or transformation. Each action would focus on the plot, lot or block as a unit of delivery:

- Individual: Single agents who wish to exercise total choice. The plot is most likely the choice of the individual although the plot could be big enough to be a full lot.

- Collective: Groups of individuals such as co-operatives. The lot or block most likely choice for these groups

- Corporate: Formal organisations such as local authorities, estates, social landlords or building companies. They would likely take on a number of lots, blocks or combinations to comprise a full phase of development.

"The Shelf House" by White Arkitekter AB, exploring a DIY, off-the-shelf approach to empower households

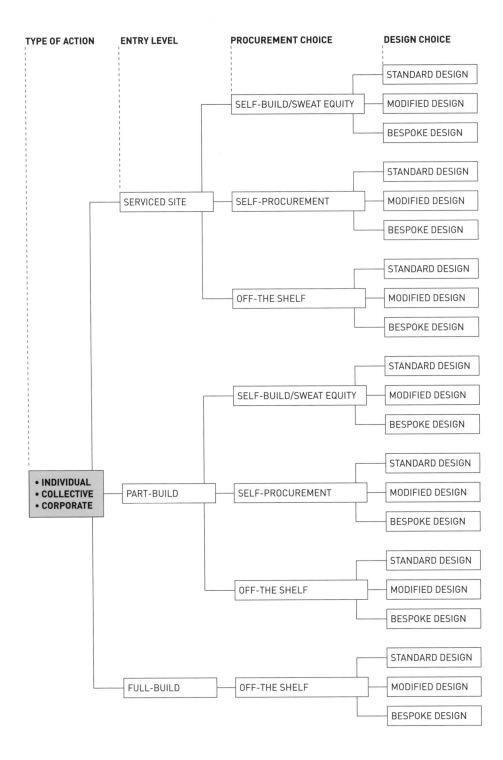

| TYPE OF ACTION | ENTRY LEVEL | PROCUREMENT CHOICE | DESIGN CHOICE |

- **INDIVIDUAL**
- **COLLECTIVE**
- **CORPORATE**

SERVICED SITE
- SELF-BUILD/SWEAT EQUITY
  - STANDARD DESIGN
  - MODIFIED DESIGN
  - BESPOKE DESIGN
- SELF-PROCUREMENT
  - STANDARD DESIGN
  - MODIFIED DESIGN
  - BESPOKE DESIGN
- OFF-THE SHELF
  - STANDARD DESIGN
  - MODIFIED DESIGN
  - BESPOKE DESIGN

PART-BUILD
- SELF-BUILD/SWEAT EQUITY
  - STANDARD DESIGN
  - MODIFIED DESIGN
  - BESPOKE DESIGN
- SELF-PROCUREMENT
  - STANDARD DESIGN
  - MODIFIED DESIGN
  - BESPOKE DESIGN
- OFF-THE SHELF
  - STANDARD DESIGN
  - MODIFIED DESIGN
  - BESPOKE DESIGN

FULL-BUILD
- OFF-THE SHELF
  - STANDARD DESIGN
  - MODIFIED DESIGN
  - BESPOKE DESIGN

Structuring complex choices around type of action, entry level, procurement and design.

ENTRY LEVEL CHOICE

Each of the types of action will trigger different choices of entry to the building process at different levels of completion:

- Serviced Site: This is the lowest level of entry and could apply to the plot, lot or block scale.

- Part Build: This involves using contractors to build the basic structure using one of the Starter Pack or Shell and Core methods.

- Full-Build: This implies a finished building to be undertaken by contractors.

PROCUREMENT CHOICE

Any of the entry levels will trigger the need to choose the method of procurement to deliver the completed building:

- Self Build/Sweat Equity: This could apply to physical involvement by individual or collectives to build out serviced sites or complete, fitout and finish part-build schemes.

- Self Procurement: This could apply to the procurement of contractors by individual or collectives to build out serviced sites or complete, fitout and finish part-build schemes.

- Off the Shelf: This implies that part-build or full-build schemes are procured as completed products built through formal organisations.

DESIGN CHOICE

Any of the above procurement choices will require decisions to be made about the preferred design route. These include:

- Standard Design: This involves the use of standard typologies which could take the form of pattern book housing.

- Modified Design: This could involve adapting standard typological approaches to offer richness and variety.

- Bespoke Design: This involves an individual personalised approach to the development of the scheme and could apply to self build/sweat equity and self procurement choices.

Our work on Making the Popular Home showed the robustness of the frontage dimension to accommodate the desired variety. It also showed that by developing different depths to the modular dimensions of the block we could accommodate a wider range of building typologies. In this way we were structuring complex choices with the potential to offer all four factors: Type of action, entry level, procurement and design route. The choice of standard or modified designs gives us the possibility of providing well-considered default settings that could be developed to the particular conditions of the place. What more do we want?

WHAT ARE THE NEW BEHAVIOURS?

Defaults give us the potential to radically change the way we deliver urban transformation whilst still ensuring compliance and consistency.

A. FOR PLANNING

The use of Neighbourhood Development Orders, linked to pattern books (and design codes) which have been developed in close collaboration with local people, provides considerable opportunities for making the policy framework for the consideration of applications for housing development more predictable. Another possibility, which would require legislation through the Localism Bill, is to introduce Planned Neighbourhood Zones. These would be areas where planning operates closer in principle to the zoning-style plans used in most continental European countries; with planning and perhaps building consent linked to one permission as long as development conforms to established rules, regulations and policies.

Such areas would be designated in development plan documents and implemented through a basic, or high level, design code with local pattern book housing. The code would guide the acceptable form and type of development without removing the freedom available to applicants to design schemes that are financially viable. Local authority discretion and the scope for public consultation could be limited because the zone would be designed with local community collaboration.

Applications for development within such zones could then be fast tracked, perhaps through a prior-notification procedure. There would also be scope to link outline permissions to such zones. Some initial pilots, prior to rolling out the programme throughout England, would enable issues to be worked through, so that they offer genuine opportunities to speed up housing delivery. To minimise disruption, it may be beneficial to introduce these in parallel with current sites allocated in plans. Another approach would be for the local authority and other public sector agencies to allocate their land, where suitable, as covered by Planned Neighbourhood Zones.

Better advice from local authorities is needed on how self-builders (and self-procurers) as well as small contractors should deal with planning applications and for simplified procedures to be introduced for small-scale developments comprised of single-unit developments or community self-build schemes. There may be a role for the self-build organisations themselves to provide assistance or information on the planning system for potential self-builders. Consideration should also be given to developing a range of approved standard house types with their modifiers. Standardisation of procedures across regulatory agencies, notably local authorities, is an important element of that.

The 'Plot, Lot and Block' principles establish an acceptable scale of development. If applicants work within this agreed principle they should get consent. Anything over this size triggers need for full planning application.

B. FOR DESIGN

With all the planning and procurement obstacles facing the individual, the small contractor or the social landlord on smaller sites, could local authorities develop their own pattern books and produce local development orders that allow approved buildings to be built anywhere in their patch? With the recent announcement of a London Housing Company, could we see a London-wide pattern book that puts into practice the ambitions of the Mayor's Housing Design Guide – with a London-wide development order? Now that would make a difference!

For designers this means focusing on the development of typological solutions at plot, lot and building scale. It involves developing the conditions to accommodate local responses or showing the potential parameters for modification by the applicant. Get this right and we now have the City of a thousand designers.

C. FOR DELIVERY

The single biggest change in the behaviour rests in the building industry and the supply chain network. Greater emphasis is needed on developing standardised solutions, modular systems and interchangeable parts.

This means:

- more research into effective mass housing construction methods;

- develop of more pattern book solutions by contractors and suppliers;

- more innovation in party wall construction and modularisation;

- development of national construction practices that work at any scale; and

- use of multi-utilities service companies as land developers.

This ultimately means a movement towards the concept of the enabling contractor who brings together both infrastructure and substructure as a combined package.

CATALYST [noun]: *An agent that stimulates or precipitates a reaction, development, or change*

CONDITION 5:
TRIGGER THE CATALYSTS

A catalyst has a greater purpose than to solve a functional problem or to provide an amenity. It involves the introduction of one ingredient to modify others. It is the stimulator of change working with the primary generators of urban form – networks and fields – to energise and open up possibilities.

In our old top-down world, catalysts were the big flagships of regeneration – the cultural project, the new bridge or public space, even the new foodstore? This would be the big idea that would trigger change and put a place on the map. This has been largely hit and miss and many places comprise of flagships only. Radical processes of transformation are changing the cities and landscapes we inhabit. The traditional instruments of architecture and urban planning are increasingly unable to address the new agenda.

In a bottom-up environment this all changes. Here, the catalyst is not a single end product but a mechanism that changes a market and impels and guides subsequent development... It is innovative and dynamic! Its purpose is the incremental, continuous generation of urban fabric. It can take non-physical forms and can be social, cultural, economic or environmental. Quite often it is as much something you do as what you do not do.

In our districts, neighbourhoods and quarters, a catalyst is anything that mobilises the energy of the massive small and fuels emergence at the local scale. They are the triggers for community formation.

DIFFUSION OF INNOVATION

Everett Rogers in his acclaimed work, 'Diffusion of Innovation', proposed that diffusion is the process by which an innovation is communicated through certain channels over time among the members of a social system. Individuals progress through 5 stages: knowledge, persuasion, decision, implementation, and confirmation. If the innovation is adopted, it spreads via various communication channels. During communication, the idea is rarely evaluated from a scientific standpoint; rather, subjective perceptions of the innovation influence diffusion. The process occurs over time. Finally, social systems determine how and what happens, the roles of opinion leaders and change agents, the types of innovation decisions, and consequences of these.

Neighbourhoods are classic self-organising systems. They form as specific clusters: around uses, activities, community groups or even social classes.

Nobody tells people where to go to, they chose to move to places that best serves their physical, social or economic needs. Every place forms its identity around its own catalysts and these are many and diverse: urban pioneers who made the first move, good schools, the best cheese shop in town, immigrant arrival points, old buildings looking for new lives. That is why creative quarters emerge around specific sectors (theatre, media, design professionals), why the lawyers go to their legal precincts, why gay neighbourhoods are colonised, why ethnic groups come together, why young families gentrify declining areas.

You cannot design these places by zoning them but you can create the conditions for them to emerge – and you can provide the catalysts to stimulate them. Catalysing any positive action, such as changing a market's perception of an area, requires an understanding of how innovation is diffused and ultimately adopted as the prevailing market view. It is now well accepted that a diffusion process in any social system follows a curved pattern in which the adoption of a new approach begins with slow change, is followed by rapid change and ends again in slow change as the product matures or new alternatives develop. People adopt innovations at different times and at different rates.

To put this into action, we need to introduce 'innovativeness' into the system. The adoption process that follows, tracked through the diffusion curve, is a decision-making process in which an individual passes from the initial knowledge of an innovation to forming an attitude toward the innovation, to a choice to adopt or reject it, then to its implementation and the use of the new idea, and finally to confirmation of this choice. In doing so, this process recognises the importance of the innovators and the early adopters in bringing the majority along.

1. INNOVATORS

Innovators are venturesome, have multiple sources of information and show greater propensity to take risks. They are motivated by the idea of being a change agent in their community. They are willing to tolerate initial problems that may accompany new approaches and are willing to make radical shifts to solving such problems.

2. EARLY ADOPTERS

They are the popular social leaders – are the visionaries in their market and are looking to adopt and use new approaches to achieve a revolutionary breakthrough that will achieve dramatic competitive advantage in their lives. They typically demand personalised solutions and quick-response, highly qualified support.

In the context of the new Localism agenda, we can take this thinking into working with communities to transform their neighbourhoods. We are not just talking about radical innovation: but any shift from the status quo will involve some form of innovation. Many people in their communities will be the agents of change. They will be the innovators or the early adopters. We need to harness their energies in our bottom-up world.

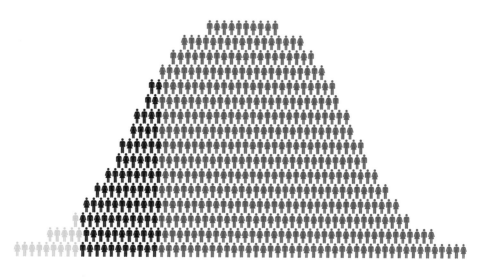

Everett Roger's 'Diffusion of Innovation' bell-curve shows the role of innovators and Early Adopters.

WHAT ARE THE CATALYSTS?

There are a number of catalysts we can consider that could trigger positive change and increase the prospects of emergence. Some involve intervention; others involve standing back. Some can be used alone or in combination with one another. All are valid:

MEANWHILE USES

The potential of meanwhile or temporary uses have long been seen as motors of urban change and it is only in recent years, through a range of successful cultural and economic projects that we can assess their true effect as catalysts. We have seen the effects of the occupations by temporary artist's colonies in places such as Soho in New York, or Temple Bar in Dublin and the regenerative effects they have had. We can also witness the success of the street market as a temporary event.

Meanwhile uses thrive in places where things have stalled and people do not know what to do. The uncertainty and openness attracts and inspires others. This has been the basis of the recent 'Meanwhile London' competition for the Royal Docks in London that looked for ideas that are exciting, will entice and attract people to the area, animate three landmark sites and transform them into great temporary 'destinations'. It also looked to promote entrepreneurial activities, create jobs for local people and encourage business start-up or incubator activities and provide opportunities for Newham's young people and local residents. The competition winners have now been announced.

Meanwhile use in Amsterdam

THE URBAN CATALYST

Studies undertaken in Berlin and other European cities through the Urban Catalyst project have shown that although meanwhile uses are thought of differently, they are important to the urban development process.

> *'Temporary uses are generally not considered to be part of normal cycles of urban development. If a building or area becomes vacant, it is expected to be re-planned, build over and used as soon as possible. Temporary uses are often associated with crisis, a lack of vision and chaos. But, despite all preconceptions, temporary uses can become an extremely successful, inclusive and innovative part of contemporary urban culture.'*

—Klaus Overmeyer

The Urban Catalyst shows that apparently spontaneous and unplanned uses revealed viable patterns and mechanisms. Meanwhile uses do not emerge accidentally but are guided by different factors and rules. The users are urban players that act deliberately and follow certain visions. The research team has come to the following conclusions, which are summarised as follows:

A   Citizens become temporary users in order to follow different aims: Users are motivated by the aim to claim vacant spaces as breeding grounds for the development of ideas, as niches or as a parallel universe in relation to the regulated urban environment.

B   Specific vacant sites attract specific meanwhile uses: While choosing certain sites or buildings, users follow precise spatial criteria such as retreat, exposure or niche.

C   Meanwhile uses flourish with a minimum of investment: These uses can recycle and appropriate existing structures and spaces with minimal interventions.

D   Meanwhile uses are mostly organised in networks and use clusters: The clusters are characterised by distinguished use profiles. A cluster is sustained by complex internal networks, which generate synergy effects. Initial temporary programs often attract similar uses to the same or a nearby site.

E   Meanwhile uses are initiated through agents: In many cases, temporary uses only become possible through the determined action of key agents, who bridge the gap between the different milieus of the users, the site owner and municipal authorities and therefore create a protective umbrella which allows for the flourishing of temporary use.

F   Meanwhile uses are a laboratory for new cultures and economies: These uses can create a unique environment of experiment, where ideas can mature in time, leading to the foundation of many start-up companies.

Without doubt, 'Meanwhile Uses' is emergence in all its forms. It only requires allowing it to happen.

INNOVATIVE LAND RELEASE STRATEGIES

It is in the creative release of land that we can make a big difference in catalysing action. Where the old ways of defining a use and marketing it for specific uses have failed it opens up the door to new thinking.

Jeroen Saris, an urban strategist from Amsterdam, has developed an interesting model for urban development in which you should have at least a period of five years to open an area, attract people with ideas and forget about strict rules. Those are the ingredients for experiments and creative development. "Development companies should not only be focused on investors, but also on ideamakers. Those idea investors should not be paid in cash, but in rights to use the space for a certain time".

FIX

A. FREE IDEA ZONES

A Free Idea Zone (FIZ) is a form of 'white land' – an unzoned part of the city – with 'fields' laid out that can be released incrementally. This is a zone where new ideas can be explored, often ideas that have not yet been fully formed and experimentation is deliberately encouraged as an innovative economic development strategy. This is emergence at its lowest level and works well in rapidly evolving economies, such as we have today.

For commercial development it is an alternative to a traditional business park model, which rigidly lays out its wares for the market to accept. Here, new companies can bite off what they need and set up at little cost to develop their offers. These are the 'fertile fields' that facilitate a form of commercial squatting that can be formalised over time. It is ideally suited to government or city development agencies and its regeneration potential is currently being explored by The London Development Agency and Newham Council in the Royal Docks area of London.

For neighbourhoods, it could be in the small trading estates on their peripheries or on former brownfield sites next to the railway tracks. In all instances it says "We are not here to tell you what to do... you tell us!"

B. GREYWORLD

Greyworld is a version of the FIZ but applied to existing underused urban fabric. It values 'messiness' – a state that defies description, but has so many possible qualities for enabling emergence. Classically it is in old industrial buildings, in spaces under the arches or in low-grade backlands. Greyworld is an economic development zone, identified in a planning document as an area where the lowest rung on the economic ladder is protected at all costs. It implies a deliberate turning of a blind eye to any activity that may arise. Staying away is a deliberate intention, particularly in keeping planners and health and safety away. This is like formalising meanwhile uses with the express intention of keeping them there.

C. TEST BEDS

This mechanism can be used to change market perception of an area and involves creative use of land to catalyse change. It involves setting aside serviced land to accommodate demonstration projects and early wins and can take the form of:

- National neighbourhood challenge pilot programmes;

- Ideas competitions where local people offer solutions that can be trialled as part of neighbourhood development projects;

- Local housing expos by local builders to test new housing models, methods and materials;

- Show home projects, either temporary or permanent that could act as benchmarks for prototyping and quality;

- Community self-build projects;

- 'Grand Designs'-type projects, working with urban pioneers and early adopters; and

- Incentive pricing of serviced land with special offers for first in, deferred land payments and discounts for early delivery.

Container City at Trinity Buoy Wharf, London

D. BAUGRUPPEN

Vauban in Freiburg, Germany has long been regarded as a good example of bottom-up urbanism. In Vauban the majority of development was by Baugruppen: small owner-cooperatives, typically comprising fewer than 20 households who want to develop and own their own houses. Part of the attraction is the opportunity, in contrast to standard speculative development, to act as a catalyst by influencing the design of their residential environment before moving in. As landowner and land developer, the Council divided land into small plots and allocated it preferentially to Baugruppen and small/local builders, with bids also being assessed against criteria favouring families with children, older people, and Freiburg residents.

FIX

Vauban's mandatory small plot sizes were significant because these allowed small developers to become involved: the largest public sector developer in the first new build phase, for example, built less than 10% – and the largest private sector developer built less than 13% – of the units. Compared to conventional housing developers, the Baugruppen approach has several distinct advantages:

- It overcomes the producer-consumer gap inherent to speculative housing and the short-termist 'in/out' behaviour of conventional developers. Combining developer and owner development roles means that the balance between upfront capital costs and longer term running costs makes energy-efficient and low-energy design more attractive. Overall costs are also lower, since Baugruppen appropriate the developer's profit.

- The Baugruppen promote community-building, cooperation and common activities between future neighbours, and enable conflict-resolution.

- The small development plots and the large proportion of new residential development built by Baugruppen (and designed by a wider variety of architects) generates a more architecturally diverse district, with the individually-designed façades creating genuine rather than artificial diversity in terms of visual character.

Baugruppen, however, need support from the City planning department and from independent consultants, and also more time to work up their proposals. Forum Vauban also formed a technical support unit.

Vauban main street in Freiburg, Germany

URBAN PIONEERS AS CATALYSTS

Urban Pioneers are Everett Rogers' innovators and early adopters. Their energy and initiative can be mobilised as potential agents of change in projects where the market is weak. This idea has its roots in the belief that many places will not be transformed into great urban living and working neighbourhoods, in the manner that we all want, if we follow the 'same-old, same-old' way. This assumes that if we follow the well-trodden path of competitive dialogue with a master developer we will not be successful.

We therefore need to find a new way to work with local people to develop a new offer and boost the local economy by building their own homes and businesses.

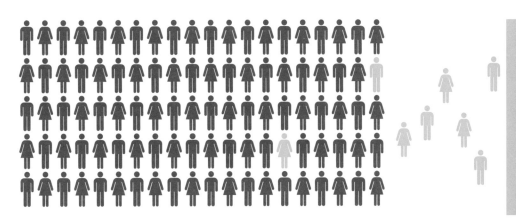

An Urban Pioneer programme can be used to stimulate a stalled housing market by initiating quick projects with a view to delivering tangible and measurable change immediately. This involves working with the innovators and fostering the early adopters in local communities and the private sector at the local level, to trial new ideas and processes. It accepts a willingness to experiment and make mistakes in the pursuit of developing better models. Using Rogers' statistics, the innovators would need to account for 2.5% and the early adopters 13.5% of the total of the total housing numbers. If we were looking for 1000 homes in the future, we would need to find 25 innovators and 135 early adopters. The Urban Pioneer programme has four phases:

PHASE 1. PHRASING THE PROPOSITION

This stage involves developing the content and branding of the proposition to create a buzz around the project – developing an early plot 'parcelling' diagram and loose design codes based on the agreed development framework for the neighbourhood and produce some early concepts to trigger interest. A steering group defines the ground rules for the project, the land release strategy, the means of delivering the programme and the risk assessment and counter-measures. As part of this process early market testing of this proposition is undertaken amongst the local creative community – working with local builders and developers to gauge its potential effectiveness. This phase sets the agenda for the longer term transformational change of the neighbourhood and provides us with the metrics for measuring its success.

PHASE 2. PROMOTING THE PROPOSITION

This stage will involve raising city-wide awareness amongst local individuals, collectives and organisations of the programme and invites them to become the 'innovators' (the 2.5%). This is done using the local press and television channels using the form of an Ideas Competition, where interested parties could express how they could take up opportunities to build their own homes or workplaces. Winners are offered plots or lots at zero cost or with some form of deferred payment and clawback conditions, provided they deliver to an agreed programme. The competition would be judged on the basis of their innovativeness as well as the commitment and ability of the successful participants to deliver on what they promise.

PHASE 3. DOCUMENTING THE PROCESS

In order to diffuse innovation to a wider audience, the programme works with local media groups to produce a documentary of the process to learn from successes and failures in the pursuit of developing better models. This could take the form of a television series based on selecting a group of 'contestants' to participate in the Programme and could be on the lines of a 'fly-on-the-wall' series. We would be looking for an ideal cross-section of 'family' and 'business' groups who best represent the neighbourhood's social, cultural and economic diversity.

PHASE 4. BUILDING THE PROJECTS

This stage involves the innovators building their projects, possibly using a 'Grand Design'-type approach to bringing together the 'contestants' with local architects and builders to build their homes and/or business units in the neighbourhood, focusing on the principle of Build Local. The projects should seek to demonstrate a wide range of responses from self-build to formal procurement, from individual to collective, from full ownership through to rental. In this way we will need to work with local social landlords, building societies and investors. Nothing should be exempt.

PHASE 5. MAKING PROGRESS

This stage will involve moving from the innovator stage to the second stage – the implementation of a further 13.5% of the total scheme to accommodate the early adopters.

The Urban Pioneer programme gives us an ideal opportunity to allow new ideas to emerge from the bottom-up. It demonstrates all the positive qualities of emergence at the local level and galvanises change. This programme is now being trialled in Middlehaven in the north of England, a place that has suffered from trying all the big solutions and where there has been a significant failure of the housing market. It is early days but its outcome could be significant for many of the stalled projects out there.

SPARKS

These are catalysts where specific higher-order generative uses or activities are introduced to trigger related activities – the civic infrastructure, public spaces and social, cultural and economic infrastructure. In other words, the 'sparks' for generating urban fabric and the local accretion of urban life:

1. LOCAL ECONOMIC CATALYSTS

The availability of affordable workspace is the single biggest catalyst for economic development at neighbourhood scale – the studios in the back lanes, space under the arches or over the shop, live/work space and the local creative industries building. This is where meanwhile uses and Greyworld can play a major role. The secret lies in ploughing the potential income streams for these activities back into other initiatives.

The success of local economic catalysts is well proven in the work of the Paddington and Shoreditch development trusts where affordable workspace is cross-funded by the councils as part of planning obligations arising out of major development projects. This has resulted in an increasing cluster of new business start-ups: an activity that has a massive impact on the local economy. The demand for this space is so great, it cannot be met.

This activity could be extended to more formal innovation hubs, enterprise centres, business incubators, accelerator programmes and mentoring schemes. In all instances these should be coupled with adjustable business rates, which could be linked to turnover.

Clockwise from top left: Enterprise space in Shoreditch; Great Western Studios in Paddington; the Kings Cross Hub; and Digital Media Hub in Dublin.

2. LOCAL SHOPPING CATALYSTS

Small, independent shops can provide a hub for communities, providing local jobs, promoting local entrepreneurial activity and keeping money circulating in the local economy. The New Economic Foundation has done a lot of work on local incentives and planned activities, recommending new ideas to counter the impacts of the major foodstores or national brands that dominate our main streets. The London Assembly's report on 'Cornered Shops' also promotes the concept of 'Shop Local'. There are now a number of schemes and initiatives where this principle has made a difference:

- Local cooperatives and buying schemes, eg. People's Supermarket;

- Community shops which could include the local Post Office;

- Local loyalty cards such as the Wedge Card or the Brixton Pound; and

- Local marketplaces, meanwhile uses and pop-up shops.

There are opportunities where zoning legislation, building on the proposition for Neighbourhood Development Zones, could promote a proportion of local independent shops on the main street to provide a balanced mix. France has excellent examples of this, where the local butcher and baker are treated as a community resource and their business rates reflect this. In all instances adjustable business rates and even devices such as tailored parking controls can be used to trigger different responses for local enterprises.

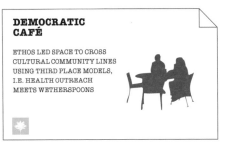

DEMOCRATIC CAFÉ

ETHOS LED SPACE TO CROSS CULTURAL COMMUNITY LINES USING THIRD PLACE MODELS, I.E. HEALTH OUTREACH MEETS WETHERSPOONS

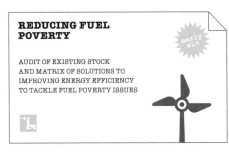

REDUCING FUEL POVERTY

early win

AUDIT OF EXISTING STOCK AND MATRIX OF SOLUTIONS TO IMPROVING ENERGY EFFICIENCY TO TACKLE FUEL POVERTY ISSUES

MICRO PLAY SPACES

UTILISING EXISTING OPEN SPACES BY ADDING SMALL SCALE INFRASTRUCTURE TO UPGRADE SPACES FOR USABLE INFORMAL USE EG BENCH, BASKET BALL HOOP

NEIGHBOURHOOD GREEN ENERGY SUPPLY

early win

NEIGHBOURHOOD WIDE COLLECTIVE PROCUREMENT TO BULK BUY CHEAPER GREENER ENERGY

ISSUE // TACKLE FUEL POVERTY ISSUES

WASTE STRATEGY

A COMBINATION OF NEW SYSTEMS AND POLICING EXISTING WASTE EG A LANDFILL TAX MODEL TO AVOID WASTE ON STREETS AND MANAGE MARKET WASTE WITH A NVAC WASTE MANAGEMENT SYSTEM TO IMPROVE THE QUALITY OF THE STREET

MECHANISMS = BORROW WEMBLEY LANDFILL TAX MODEL, WORK WITH VEOLIA ENVIRONMENTAL SERVICES ON DEVELOPING A NVAC WASTE MANAGEMENT

STREET AS COMMUNITY ORCHARD

INTRODUCE FRUIT TREE PLANTING AS A CO-CREATION EVENT TO SEED OWNERSHIP AND RECLAIMING PUBLIC REALM

MECHANISMS = SUPPORT AND EXTEND THE EXISTING GROW BAG SCHEME IN PENFOLD STREET.

Sparks as catalysts to neighbourhood change [Urban Initiatives and 00:/ architecture, 2009]

3. NEIGHBOURHOOD MANAGEMENT AS A CATALYST

Having a dedicated management team for the neighbourhood is one of the most effective means of triggering transformation of the area. The National Association of Neighbourhood Management sees neighbourhood management as residents working in partnership with mainstream service providers, the local authority, businesses and the voluntary and community sectors, to make local services more responsive to the needs of their area. It is a process that recognises the uniqueness of each place; allowing the people that live, work or provide services in it to build on its strengths and address its specific challenges.

Operating in a defined area and at a scale that people identify with, and crucial to its success is the neighbourhood manager; advocate, mediator, facilitator, influencer and negotiator for positive change. It does not involve large amounts of money – rather using existing resources in a better way. This is well demonstrated through the work of the Church Street Management Team in London, which has provided the catalyst to the development of its Neighbourhood Plan; its extensive public art and cultural programmes; and the management of its street market.

The role of the neighbourhood management could be extended to the management of hardware projects, taking on the co-ordination of new housing and infrastructure programmes. This could see planning contributions directed to revenue funding for local management. This could be complemented by rents received from local managed workspace.

4. COMMUNITY OWNERSHIP AS A CATALYST

The catalytic effect of well-managed physical assets, such as community and faith centres, parks, and redundant buildings, are well recognised in the development of active communities and viable community-based enterprises. Asset transfer, a well rehearsed principle in local politics, refers to local communities' ability to acquire land and buildings, either at market value or at a discount, in order to deliver services that meet the neighbourhood's needs. It is seen as one way in which local authorities in particular, can support the development of the social economy, and thereby meet their wider strategies for renewal and improved delivery of local services.

Indy Johar's work on 'Scale Free Schools' points to the need for a different approach to the provision of school buildings and services. Why can't the whole community become the 'school', with just a central core and then just activate underutilised buildings and resources to build a strong sense of community? In this way schools can scale up or scale down to meet the community's needs and not treat learning as a 'factory' process. This could extend to developing a central booking system to make all of our underused buildings work more effectively.

Our work on 'Start with the Park' for CABE showed the benefits of community ownership in developing and maintaining green spaces. Places that are 'owned' are places that are loved.

5. INFRASTRUCTURE TRIGGERS

The provision of new local energy networks, district wide heating systems, sustainable urban drainage schemes and retrofitting projects provides a ready catalyst for neighbourhood transformation.

The 'Future is Local' report by the Sustainable Development Commission shows that there is an unrealised opportunity in Britain to catalyse this potential by focusing on the neighbourhood as the optimum scale for addressing infrastructure reinvestment needs. At neighbourhood scale:

- Engagement of residents can be secured through governance approaches most appropriate to each community and providing the supply chain and investors with a viable scale of project and structure of partner;

- Efficiency measures become feasible at whole-street and neighbourhood level that simply don't stack up at individual home scale, including most low-carbon/renewable energy technologies and transport;

- Access to private investment is increased as neighbourhood scale provides 'critical mass', enabling scarce public money to be more effectively leveraged.

We now need practical solutions – the 'how' of managing upgrade works on a neighbourhood basis. This requires building capacity at local level, developing and sharing best practice nationally and facilitating engagement by supply chain businesses, funders and policy-makers wishing to see communities successfully taking ownership for changing the place they live.

6. SOFT CATALYSTS

Neighbourhoods are often recognised as the places where the dynamics of social cohesion are most tangible within the city. Within the overall urban dynamics, neighbourhoods have also been the breeding grounds for socio-economic development projects, grassroots initiatives and social innovation, especially in the social economy. Not all triggers need to be hardware. Sometimes softer catalysts such as empowerment of the community through neighbourhood planning programmes, civic leadership and capacity building initiatives can have a greater lasting effect on neighbourhood transformation. This extends to:

- social enterprise activities;

- greening projects and urban orchards;

- social and cultural programmes;

- neighbourhood watch; and

- social network developments.

One of the best examples of soft catalysts is access to seed finance at the local level: micro-finance to set up local businesses; community banks and credit unions; and, local guarantee funds for community self-build schemes.

NEIGHBOURHOOD CO:EFFICIENT

Neighbourhood Coefficient is a method for refining the 'Catalysts' for Smart Urbanism to make massive small change at the local level. It is an operating system that optimises the hardware of the neighbourhood – its land, buildings, infrastructure, networks and spaces – to run its software – the human needs of enterprise, social capital, shelter and marketplace. This recognises the need for innovation into new ways to deliver local services, provide new infrastructure and manage local change. We know that we must move to new ways of delivering flexible housing choice and tenure in our neighbourhoods. We also know that we can only meet some of our carbon reduction challenges if we address these at neighbourhood scale.

The Sustainable Development Commission has found that enabling communities to lead local renewal projects with a neighbourhood scale approach is the most cost-effective way to ensure towns and cities are fit for the future and create the conditions for people to thrive. Through empowering community groups to come together to tackle issues of local priority, and to work in partnership with local authorities and businesses, multiple benefits can be delivered. Upgrades to our physical infrastructure can tackle climate change, deliver reliable and efficient transport networks, improve health and well being, secure a healthy natural environment, improve long-term housing supply, maximise employment opportunities, and make our communities safer and more cohesive.

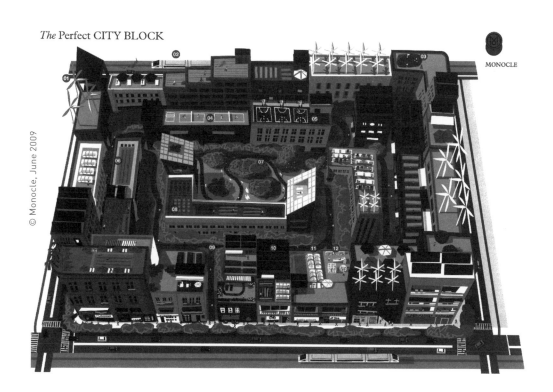

The Perfect CITY BLOCK

MONOCLE

© Monocle, June 2009

Monocle's view of the ideal neighbourhood

Neighbourhood Coefficient is intended as a 'pilot project' approach aimed at delivering targeted funds directly to neighbourhoods to unlock new thinking, processes and outcomes in the planning, design and delivery of our neighbourhoods. It is based on stimulating a stalled housing market by initiating quick projects with a view to delivering tangible and measurable change immediately while other more radical changes are implemented by the government. This involves working with local communities to trial new ideas and accepts a willingness to experiment and make mistakes in the pursuit of developing better models. The range of new models to be explored should include:

1. POPULAR HOME PROJECTS

Pattern books comprising new long life, loose fit housing typologies could be further developed to reflect the uniqueness of a place and offer the widest range tenures and lifetime choice. These must allow for incremental approaches to housing design using 'starter packs' to challenge established house-building approaches, space standards, affordable housing criteria and entry levels to the housing market. It should also consider innovative approaches to housing construction including development of modern methods to ensure effective economies of scale in all our work, taking advantage of normative approaches to housing design, mass construction techniques and joint utilities provision. This model could apply to many small underutilised sites in our towns and cities where planning obstacles could be overcome though use of pattern books allied to Local Development Orders.

2. LOCAL DELIVERY VEHICLES

Development of innovative neighbourhood-scale organisational structures and delivery vehicles that can be adapted to the special requirements of a place, the community and the Council are critical to the success of any neighbourhood project. The model focuses on alternative approaches to long-term control of land; long-term investment models; risk-sharing and joint ventures with the Council; as well as financing models that will ensure continued management, stewardship and maintenance of the neighbourhood. As part of this programme we should be trialling Community Land Trusts and other innovations around land release, deferred land costs, private rental housing to stimulate the full range of responses locally.

3. LOCAL ENERGY SOLUTIONS

Development of funding, implementation and management packages to set up local energy services and retrofitting companies to meet the low carbon challenge. This model should be delivered on a flexible and incremental basis ensuring that the full benefits of a local approach are realised at the lowest thresholds of the community and the Council can share in its returns without exposing itself to undue levels of risk. Benefits include reduced cost and disruption; engaging communities; and unlocking smarter finance linked to long-term revenue streams. It proposes an environmental dimension to the Big Society agenda, and a clear vision for the drive to localism.

FIX

4. INNOVATION AROUND NEIGHBOURHOOD SERVICES

Development of processes to draw together all service providers in a single and focused approach to ensure effective and scaleable neighbourhood infrastructure and services are delivered. This should extend to maximising the use of community assets through local 'booking' systems and co-ordinating local procurement of goods and services to realise social innovation and public good outcomes for the neighbourhood. Critical to active collaboration is the need for innovative approaches around community mobilisation and the use of community charters, local agreements and new social contracts – 'We will, if you will'. As part of this programme we should look to new forms of revenue finance to maintain the long-term future of 'software' projects that foster community action and responsibility.

5. SOCIAL ENTERPRISE MODELS

Development of a range of innovative approaches in diverse and complex neighbourhoods to building social capital and fostering local economic development through micro-economic initiatives, community enterprise and links to training providers. This should extend to development of local building companies; partnerships with local contractors and local building suppliers; and local apprentice schemes to ensure that the social and economic benefits of new housing construction and community retrofitting are realised locally.

6. FLEXIBLE PROCUREMENT PROCESSES

Development of flexible, targeted and incremental land release strategies that deliver serviced land to the market at a range of scales – the individual plot for self-builders and those seeking bespoke solutions; the 'lot' (a collection of plots) that could involve a small number of units to be built by local small builders and social landlords; the urban block that could open opportunities for larger local contractors and agencies; to the whole phase that could entice the national housebuilders. This process could allow the full range of catalysts and creative land release strategies for a range of players.

Neighbourhood Co:efficient offers some useful ideas but it also brings with it serious challenges. We know that in addition to the recognised planning obstacles for the small builder or the self-procurer, access to affordable land represents the single biggest limiter to multiple small actions at the neighbourhood scale. This is where we need to be really innovative. Land release does not necessarily mean land sale, or if it does, it does not mean freehold. If it does, it does not necessarily mean that payment cannot be deferred. It is now accepted that more flexible approaches are essential.

The Mayor of London has announced that his publicly owned land should be used to unlock the housing bottleneck, using innovative methods. There is no reason for all local authorities to unlock their hidden stashes and follow suit.

RUNNING A PILOT PROGRAMME

Three courses of action are needed:

1. DEVELOP A STARTER PACK
This requires a basic set of rules to start the process and providing the management to get it up and running and evolve it.

- **The Rules of Engagement** – Setting out clearly defined roles and responsibilities of all players.

- **The Project Programme** – Agreeing key milestones and deliverables throughout the programme

- **The Definition of Success** – Clearly spelling out the criteria to reward successful innovation

2. ESTABLISH A HIT SQUAD
This can be an extension of the local authority operating as a dedicated interim management team until a fully-fledged delivery vehicle is in place. It covers the key roles of all players:

- **The Project Initiator** – Focus on early wins and manage highly visible projects such as building show-homes, demonstration projects and active community participation in integrating new communities.

- **The Development Packager** – Breaking the project down into bite-size chunks to enable a wider range of implementation strategies.

- **The Place Promoter** – Providing the branding, communications and marketing functions for the programme.

- **The Supporter** – Provide support throughout the process on such matters as legal, procurement and policy implications.

- **The Programme Coordinator** – Providing the necessary client-side project management and costs control.

- **The Capacity Builder** – Working with the Council and neighbourhood team to raise standards, focus efforts and leave behind an intellectual legacy.

3. MONITOR THE PROCESS
This involves establishing a basic set of rules to monitor the process and providing the management the tools to review and evaluate its success over time. It also includes:

- creating the mechanisms to share ideas to a wider audience;

- setting up feedback loops;

- redefining strategy on an ongoing basis; and

- reporting on progress and lessons learnt.

HOW SHOULD IT BE FUNDED?

We think the government should set up a programme of pilot projects similar to City Challenge in the 1990s, which directs funding directly to the neighbourhoods over a sustained period, with continued funding linked to successful public good outcomes. City Challenge had some success but it was too widely drawn and too top-down driven. Notwithstanding this, it was one of the better programmes. We can learn from this and allow more freedom for the detailed objectives of the programme to be developed at the local level.

The programme should identify targets and these could be, say:

1   First projects by a certain date to force action

2   Quantum of new homes by a certain date

3   Number of local jobs created by a certain date

4   Public good outcomes and social impacts, and

5   National Exhibition in say, five years

The Neighbourhood Coefficient initiative offers a strong brand and creates a 'buzz'. It will promote more experimental and high visibility projects that will capture the imagination of politicians and the wider community by addressing the issues of social inclusiveness, environmental concerns and cultural diversity, amongst others.

WHAT ARE THE NEW BEHAVIOURS?

Many of the methods outlined in this chapter require fundamentally different modes of behaviour, particularly by the public sector, in the planning, design and delivery of catalytic projects. In a constantly evolving programme of change, we need to set aside our obsessions with neatness and accept 'messiness' as a precursor to emergence.

A. FOR PLANNING

Here we embrace the informal. We accept flux as an emergent condition prior to maturity. We are prepared to turn a blind eye and give it time to settle. We now manage it better. We arm a place with its triggers of change. We monitor and adapt.

Despite the obvious fundamental contradiction between planned and unplanned the informal and the formal are not contradictions. Saskia Sassen's studies on global economies and world cities shows that informal and formal economies not only coexist but also depend on each other.

While innovation comes more from informal contexts, formal contexts ensure normally long lasting, sustainable effects. This means we must formalise the informal. This is needed to analyse and understand the unplanned patterns behind self-organised activities, deduct prototypes, models and tools from these investigation, formalise them and make them available to all stakeholders. One the other hand, formal procedures of planning, administration and management have to be critically examined and ways and strategies to be found, how existing practices can be de-formalised, de-institutionalised, adapted and changed.

We throw away our obsession with evidence that looks backward, open our eyes and plan instinctively. Like in Vauban, planners are liberated to plan!

B. FOR DESIGN

Catalysts open up the potential for unlimited innovation in all its forms. Design becomes more local, more personal and more exciting. We use our urban pioneers to initiate and mobilise change. Innovation is king. The others follow. There is a greater focus on experimentation in a range of locations. Design becomes relevant again!

C. FOR DELIVERY

It is the context of many of the land release methods discussed in this chapter that behaviours will need to change. This includes changing or bending the rules on land sales by the public sector, on procurement rules and on the nature of ownership. Rigid procurement rules are an obstacle to a more flexible approach.

Gap funding, as a catalyst is not likely to be available for some years, but improving financial viability and reducing risk can nevertheless be improved with the assistance of the public sector in a number of ways:

- Deferring payment for the land until the completion of the scheme or building. There is already an understanding in the public sector that land value can be deferred.

- Adopting a long leasehold approach with a ground rent arrangement, which could be bought out by the developer or a succeeding owner paying a premium at any point during the lease. The ground rent could be inflation-proofed by regular rent reviews.

- Converting land value into a share in the ownership of the property with the developer or succeeding owner having the option to purchase at a later date at then market value.

- Promoting self-build for commercial or residential property has the potential to widen the benefits a developer can enjoy.

- Reducing the build costs by using the purchasing power of the Local Authority or other government agencies to reduce build costs.

- Providing financial guarantees to assist small local developers secure development finance.

- Considering joint ventures with the private sector to share the risk and the profit.

- Focusing on smaller sites and being prepared to look at anything from a single house plot upwards. Nothing is too small.

- Being pro-active on infrastructure and utilities.

It is around using catalysts that we can make the biggest difference.
This is where we need to trial new methods and build up our toolkits.
Experimentation (without fear of failure) is imperative if we are to change.

Without leaps of imagination, or dreaming,
we lose the excitement of possibilities.
Dreaming, after all, is a form of planning.

—Gloria Steinem

EPILOGUE

Every year at MIPIM, cities lay out their wares. Every city declares its vision for its future. All strive to be bigger and better. All use the same techniques: "Look at our tall buildings – we have a Foster tower, a Calatrava bridge, a Martha Schwartz public space!". In trying to differentiate, they all become the same. They are all selling an end state that may never be realised. What would happen if a city said, "Look at our possibilities!"?

When Clive Dutton, in his previous role as Director of Planning and Regeneration in Birmingham, commissioned Urban Initiatives to produce the Big City Plan, he had a mantra. He wanted a plan that would 'never be finished'. In doing so he was embracing the view that he was looking to create the conditions for emergence not to dictate an end state. Birmingham was perfectly poised for such an approach. It had the urban fabric that was adaptive to change. It had all the generators in place. It just needed the essential diagram and the simple rules to release the city of a thousand designers – something it had started with its growth as an world economic powerhouse and reshaped with the Highbury Initiative some twenty years ago. In the thinking of the Big City Plan we were talking about keeping the planners (and health and safety) away from certain areas to foster economic development at the lowest levels. We wanted to create the 'Birmingham House' as the smallest unit of design and delivery for new people living in the city centre. We wanted to create the conditions to allow the formation of new districts, neighbourhoods and quarters. We wanted an essential and simple structure that would foster emergence. This approach was in conflict with those obsessed with certainty and the end state –through a planning system so driven by looking backwards that it could not see forwards.

Clive was on to something and took this thinking with him when he went to Newham. Since then we have explored with him the concepts of 'Free Ideas Zones' in the Royal Docks, and the 'Spark' in Stratford – both ways of exploring emergence and convergence in the context of an economic strategy for East London. Urban Initiatives' work in preparing the Stratford Metropolitan Masterplan follows a plot-based approach to allowing massive small change. The entire plan can be subdivided to the smallest scale, upscaled or downscaled to allow infinite possibilities.

Smart Urbanism moves away from the same old 'place making' agenda to that of 'condition making' - a new approach to planning, designing and delivering sustainable urbanism and social innovation in our districts, neighbourhoods and quarters. It is how urban design must change in this new world.

We have developed and tested this approach in a number of projects in recent years: the Aylesbury Estate in south London, Scotswood Neighbourhood in Newcastle, and in Luton High Town. We are now using the Smart Urbanism 'tools' as a way of forming a new neighbourhood in Middlehaven, with an urban pioneers' programme at its heart. We are testing the proposal for a London-wide MASSIVE SMALL initiative with the idea of a pilot programme in those boroughs who want to innovate around the use of their land. With 140,000 new homes planned for the capital, London must lead the way. The rest of the world is watching. The Mayor's Housing Design Guide gives us the agenda and the purpose. In all these instances, the tools are working. They just make common sense.

The recently announced Enterprise Zones offer a real opportunity for new thinking. Without this we will get it wrong again. The last round of enterprise zones started the trend to bigness. "Build it big and jobs will come" they said. In many instances no-one came. Some came, saw and left. What was left was the legacy of the top-down megastructures – the Europarks, the flagships, the architectural zoos. In other words, the very things that threatened good urbanism. We don't need big architecture... just big ideas.

If Enterprise Zones are truly about economic development and not just about property development, then they must be about widening opportunity to many players. In Middlehaven, now designated as a new Enterprise Zone on Teeside, we are testing lot-based urbanism as a way of opening up access to local entrepreneurs. In the Royal Docks, also recently designated, the big-bang business park model has never delivered. What is needed here is a Free Ideas Zone to allow experimentation. Create a thousand lots and allow many things to happen. Keep a light hand on the tiller and actively manage and monitor change. Try things! If we do it right we can get it right. Thinking MASSIVE SMALL is the key!

Smart Urbanism: London is now formed with MASSIVE SMALL as its polemic. We want to push it as a learning and action-based research and development agenda. This is the time for us to be innovating. We cannot wait!

Remember, the masterplan is not dead in a bottom-up world. It becomes even more important - but must take different forms. It must now be more suggestive rather than prescriptive. We cannot dictate end states but we can release the ingenuity of collective thinking of man if we put the right conditions in place. If the processes and behaviours that are the essence of planning, design and delivery are to change to respond to the new agenda, the masterplan must look to the lightest touch, not the heavy hand of control.

The masterplan now becomes the 'microplan' – the means of enabling MASSIVE SMALL.

Have a bias toward action – let's see something happen now. You can break that big plan into small steps and take the first step right away.

—Indira Gandhi

BIBLIOGRAPHY

The first thing that surprised me was how little original thinking has taken place in the sphere of urbanism in recent years but how much we can draw from other sources in other fields of endeavour. The old theorists are still the best ones and are probably more relevant today than ever, so I have drawn extensively on their great work which still challenges us to think differently. The Web makes it easy to find all of the books, journals and articles I refer to in this book so, taking a clue from John Maeda's book The Laws of Simplicity (2006), I have avoided the practice of a bibliographic entry for each item. Rather, I list these below as valuable source material and inspiration:

THEOREM

- Re:Urbanism by Kelvin Campbell and Rob Cowan (2002): The book that kicked this all off and still rings true.

- Motivation and Personality by Abraham Maslow (1970): What really motivates us.

- Technics and Civilisation by Lewis Mumford (1963): Words ahead of the time.

- Life and Death in American Cities by Jane Jacobs (1961): The old lady knew more than we realised

- New Theory of Urban Design by Christopher Alexander (1987): Still a benchmark for thinking about urban design

- The Long Tail by Chris Anderson (2006); The editor of Wired magazine with his finger on the button

- The New Economy by Kevin Kelly (2007): On the power of social networks.

- Total Politics by Greg Clark (2003): A critique of centralised government.

- The Politics of Universal Compassion by Joel Federman (2002): On cynicism and optimism in modern life.

- Small is Beautiful by EF Schumacher (1973): A study of economics as if people mattered

BROKEN

- Plandemonium by Rob Cowan (2010): Brilliant insight into the failure of modern planning

- Clone Towns Report by New Economics Foundation (2004): The state of our high streets.

- Red Tory by Philip Blond (2008): Good rant on the failure of centralism.

- A Guide to the New Ruins of Great Britain by Owen Hatherly (2010): Our Pevsner for the 21st century.

- Adaptable Buildings by Alex Lipshutz (2007): Article in Adaptable Architecture

- The Manual for Streets 2 (2010): Getting there but still not enough.

- The Regeneration Crisis by Steve Tolson (2008): Really good paper that spells out the costs of procurement

- Death of Common Sense by Philip Howard (1995): The truths behind unintended consequences.

- Incrementalism is the Key by Paul Finch (December 2010) Editorial comment in Architect's Journal

THINKING

- Emergence, The Connected lives of Ants, Brains and Cities by Steven Johnson (2001): Great insight into self organising systems. Probably the best on emergent urbanism.

- The Tipping Point by Malcolm Gladwell (2002): When does the paradigm shift.

- The Laws of Simplicity by John Maeda (2006): Keeping it simple

- Disabling Professions by Ivan Illich (1978): Reminds us why we need to change.

- Notes on the Synthesis of Form by Christopher Alexander (1964): Ideas on generative methods in architecture.

- The Dictionary of Urbanism by Rob Cowan (2005): Where you can always find insight and humour.

- Wisdom of Crowds by James Surowiecki (2004): the power of the group.

- Conceptualizing The Principles of Emergent Urbanism by Mathieu Hélie (2009): Flying the banner for emergence.

- The Emergence Of Cities: Complexity And Urban Dynamics by Michael Batty (2003): The mechanics of emergence

- What is Complexity Science, really? By Steven Phelan (2004): Getting back to the real science.

- Emergence: From Chaos to Order by John Holland (1998): Cities as patterns in time.

- Smart Swarm by Peter Miller (2010): How we can learn from nature.

- The Paradox of Choice by Barry Schwartz (2005): Why less choice is more.

- Nudge by Cass Sunstein and economist Richard Thaler (2008): How to structure complex choices

- Whatever Happened to Urbanism by Rem Koolhaas (1995): Pure reductionism

- Town and Town-making Principles by Andres Duany (2000): Setting out the stall for a new urbanism.

- Generative methods in Urban Design by Michael Mehaffy (2003): Christopher Alexander versus the New Urbanists.

FIX

Condition 1. Simple Rules
- General Urban Rules by Alex Lehnerer (2009): A valuable sourcebook for method rules as tools in urban design.

- Urban Renaissance Towns by Alan Simpson (2007): Charters as collaborative tools.

- Public Protocol by Urban Initiatives (2010): A neighbourhood planning toolkit.

Condition 2. Intelligent Networks
- A City is not a Tree by Christopher Alexander (1979): Thinking in semi-lattices.

- Streetgrids as Frameworks for Urban Variety by Paul Groth (1976): Making a case for grids

- Structuring a Generative Model for Urban Design by Beirão and Duarte (2007): Using computers to generate urban fabric.

- Space is the Machine by Bill Hillier (1999): From science to application.

- Urban ISM by Urban Initiatives (2009): A platform for integrated spatial modelling.

Condition 3. Emergent Fields
- Making of the Modern Street by Group 91 (1999): How to subdivide for urban grain.

- Housing Design Guide by Design for London and Urban Initiatives Team (2010): Calling for the new Georgian.

- Cityplan as Resource by Jonathan Smyth (1989): Plotting the change in Savannah over the years.

- Anatomy of the Village by Tom Sharp (1946): The tradition of Scottish town-making.

- The New Norm by Urban Initiatives (2008): Towards a lot-based urbanism.

Condition 4. Standard Defaults
- Diffusion of Innovation by Everett Rogers (1997): How to change a market.

- What Home Buyers Want by CABE (2007): Stated preferences from housing market

- Housing Audit by CABE (2006): The state of housing design in the UK.

- Towards a New Vernacular by Mark Parsons (1998): A good trot through the preconditions for delivering better housing.

- An Introduction to Housing Layout by the Greater London Council (1972): The last seen pattern book in London

- Housey Housey by Pierre d'Avoine (2005): Making the case for a return to pattern book housing.

- Supports: An Alternative to Mass Housing by John Habraken (1972): Open building at different levels.

- Design Codes by Carmona and Dann (2007): The pros and cons.

- The Future of Residential Development' by Knight Frank (2009): State of the housing market in the UK.

- The Housebuilding Industry: Promoting Recovery in Housing Supply by University of Reading for the Department of Local Government and Communities (2009): Points to the need for diversification

- The Popular Home by Urban Initiatives (2010): Demonstrating a new approach to long-life, loose fit homes.

Condition 5. Trigger the Catalysts
- Urban Catalyst by Klaus Overmeyer (2009): Using urban pioneers to as an alternative development model.

- Delivering Better Places by the Scottish Government (2010): A sourcebook for planning, design and delivery models.

- Building Social Capital by Indy Johar (2005): Making better neighbourhoods.

- Start with the Park by Urban Initiatives for CABE (2006): Showing the catalytic effect of green spaces.

- The Future is Local by the Sustainable development Commission (2010): Effective scales for infrastructure delivery.

- Neighbourhood Co:efficient by Urban Initiatives (2009): Defining the catalysts for neighbourhood transformation.

NOTES